Italic Letters

CALLIGRAPHY & HANDWRITING

Inga Dubay & Barbara Getty

VNR VAN NOSTRAND REINHOLD COMPANY
NEW YORK CINCINNATI TORONTO LONDON MELBOURNE

To Joe & Glenn, with love

Printed in the United States of America

Designed by Inga Dubay and Barbara Getty

Published by Van Nostrand Reinhold Company Inc.
135 West 50th Street
New York, New York 10020

Van Nostrand Reinhold Company Limited
Molly Millars Lane
Wokingham, Berkshire RG11 2PY, England

Van Nostrand Reinhold
480 La Trobe Street
Melbourne, Victoria 3000, Australia

Macmillan of Canada
Division of Gage Publishing Limited
164 Commander Boulevard
Agincourt, Ontario M1S 3C7, Canada

16 15 14 13 12 11 10 9 8 7 6 5 4 3 2 1

Library of Congress Cataloging in Publication Data

Dubay, Inga.
   Italic letters.

   Bibliography: p.
   Includes index.
   1. Writing, Italic—Handbooks, manuals, etc.
2. Calligraphy—Handbooks, manuals, etc. I. Getty,
Barbara. II. Title.
Z43.D78 1984   745.6'1977   83-1235
ISBN 0-442-22806-6 (pbk.)

CONTENTS

FOREWORD

We have written this book hoping you will enjoy italic writing – enjoy the beautiful letterforms, enjoy the feeling of ink on paper, enjoy the growth of your own italic script.

The letters in this book are our own version of italic patterned after our study of historical manuscripts and the models of Lloyd Reynolds. Work with our models; trace and copy them until you know and feel the letters. Your own style in both the formal and handwriting versions will develop as you progress through the book. Your own unique personality will add rhythm and vitality to these letters.

The writing exercises in this book – aside from providing an opportunity for improving your skills – offer a brief overview of the historical tradition of the written letter. Other related facts may be found in the marginal notes.

The current revival of calligraphy and craftsmanship began with William Morris and continued with Edward Johnston. In our day, italic was furthered by Alfred Fairbank & Lloyd Reynolds. The work of Charles Lehman, Tom Gourdie, and Irene Wellington has contributed to today's interest in italic handwriting.

Our teachers and colleagues, Jacqueline Svaren and the late Lois McClelland, together with many others, are a part of this continuing calligraphic tradition.

This book is a tool for you – use it and enjoy!

We especially want to thank our husbands and sons ·

ΛBC·Uncial ABC·Half-uncial abc·Carolingian abc·Gothic abc·Humanistabc·Italic abc

·Egyptian 𓃾(A)·⬚(A)·Phoenician ∀ ᴼˣ ALEPH·ᕼ house BETH·ᔑ camel GIMEL·Early Greek ΑΔ ALPHA·ꓭ Β BETA·ᐅ⟨ GAMMA·Classical Greek

CHAPTER I

How
to Use
this Book

·Basic Italic Aa Bb Cc·Formal Italic Aa Bb Cc·Cursive Italic Aan Bbn Ccn·

ITALIC CALLIGRAPHY AND HANDWRITING

Italic is a modern writing system derived from 16th–century letterforms that began in Italy and later were used in Europe and England. They are simple, yet elegant letters that may be written as an art form in formal italic calligraphy or as a rapid, legible everyday hand-writing.

BASIC ITALIC HANDWRITING
MONOLINE TOOL AND EDGED PEN
Basic Italic Lower-case Letters and
Capital Letters (Chapters II and III)

The qualities of letterforms
at their best are order,
simplicity and grace.

D. W. DWIGGINS

FORMAL ITALIC CALLIGRAPHY
EDGED PEN
Formal Italic Lower-case Letters and
Capital Letters (Chapters V and VI)

CALLIGRAPHY
is distinguished
by harmony of style.

A. E. LOWE

CURSIVE ITALIC HANDWRITING
MONOLINE TOOL
Cursive Italic Handwriting (Chapter VIII)

True ease in writing
comes from art, not chance,
and those move easiest
who have learned to dance.

ALEXANDER POPE

CURSIVE ITALIC HANDWRITING
EDGED PEN
Cursive Italic Handwriting (Chapter VIII)

Letters are symbols
which turn matter
into spirit.

ALPHONSE DE LAMARTINE

"Calligraphy," from the Greek KALLI (beautiful) and GRAPHIA (writing), generally refers to letters handwritten with a mono-line or edged tool. "Lettering" usually refers to letters drawn with many strokes and often filled in.

Italic calligraphy is presented in this book in a do-it-yourself format. Basic, formal & cursive italic are introduced first with the monoline tool and then with the edged pen. The mono-line tool will provide a single-width line throughout the letter; the edged pen will lend a handsome, chiseled appearance to your writing.

This is written
with a monoline tool.

This is written
with an edged pen.

This book will help you attain a flowing calligraphic hand. You will need to purchase a few simple supplies, but your most expensive investment will be your time — spend it wisely and you'll bring yourself and others pleasure through your writing.

Handwriting is one of the tools of learning. In American schools the general practice in the primary grades has been to introduce a drawn manuscript alphabet usually referred to as ball and stick. These letterforms require exceptional motor co-ordination in order for the student to form circles and straight lines. Rhythmic move-ment, the essential nature of handwriting, is ignored.

BALL AND STICK
(many lifts)

ITALIC
(few lifts)

one stroke – no lifts

Then about the time the student is beginning to master these forms, usually in the third grade, commercial (looped) cursive is introduced. Often children become confused and frustrated when confronted with learning the commercial cursive capitals and lower-case letters that change form & have added loops.

BALL AND STICK TO COMMERCIAL CURSIVE

b	becomes	*b*	e	becomes	*e*
f	becomes	*f*	z	becomes	*z*
A	becomes	*a*	F	becomes	*F*
G	becomes	*G*	Q	becomes	*2*
S	becomes	*S*	T	becomes	*T*

Most people educated in the United States experienced this drastic change in handwriting forms. As a result, many adults are dissatisfied with their everyday hand. Many adults print in all capitals, write a mixture of a print script and looped cursive, or script that resembles italic (elliptical in nature with no loops).

SOME PEOPLE PRINT
IN ALL CAPS.

Some others mix
cursive and printing.

And yet others write
in a form that
resembles italic.

Since people often experience difficulty in reading the hand-writing of others—and sometimes their own—in the United States the writer generally is requested to "please print."

This book offers you an alter-native — italic handwriting. Follow our step-by-step method to a legible, handsome everyday hand.

7

WRITING IN THIS BOOK

ITALIC LETTERS: CALLIGRAPHY AND HANDWRITING has been designed to provide a self-instructional course in basic, formal, chancery & cursive italic.

Read Chapter I and obtain the necessary writing tools. As you begin Chapter II, study the comments at the top of the page and in the margin.

Select the proper writing tool, read a line of writing, and trace the model letters. Then copy them directly on the book page in the space provided below. Do WRITE IN THIS BOOK!

The first image is the model letter. The second image has arrows to indicate the number and direction of strokes. On line 1 trace the second and third images of each letter. On line 2 trace the dotted image, then write your own letters.

Tracing the model letters on the page before writing below them may give you an awareness of finger and hand movements that will help you form the proper letter shapes.

When writing in this book, use a colored – rather than black – ink. Your work will then stand out, and you can easily compare it with the model.

At the back of the book you will find sample ruled pages. These may be removed and duplicated for further practice, or these guide sheets may be placed under a blank sheet of white paper for additional practice space. You may also wish to use tracing paper to copy the book page.

When writing, start all letters at the top, then go down or over to the left or right. (The exception is lower-case d, which begins on the waist line.) Follow the directional arrows that accompany the models.

One arrow indicates a one-stroke letter with no lift of the writing tool.

Two arrows indicate a two-stroke letter with one lift of the writing tool.

Note:
When practicing letters on your own, write a letter 3 times only. Writing a line of 1 letter is of little value. As soon as possible, write words and sentences – put your writing to use!

STYLES OF ITALIC

Four styles of writing are presented in this book.

BASIC ITALIC (Chapters II and III), print-script writing without serifs, is introduced with the monoline tool and edged pen.

Basic Italic **Basic Italic**
monoline tool   edged pen

FORMAL ITALIC (Chapters V and VI), unjoined writing with serifs, is presented with the edged tool.

(The monoline tool is used for introductory practice only in Chapters V and VI. Formal italic is generally written with the edged pen.)

Formal Italic
edged pen

CHANCERY ITALIC (Chapter VII), flourished writing with serifs, is presented with the edged pen.

(Chancery italic is generally written with the edged pen only.)

Chancery Italic
edged pen

CURSIVE ITALIC (Chapter VIII), joined handwriting with serifs, is presented with the monoline tool and the edged pen.

Cursive Italic Handwriting
monoline tool

Cursive Italic Handwriting
edged pen

LOWER-CASE FAMILIES

Lower-case letters are presented in family groups according to similar shapes.

FAMILY 1
Letters with downstrokes:

i j l   i j l
monoline   edged pen

FAMILY 2
Letters with diagonals:

k v w x z   k v w x z

FAMILY 3
Letters with arches:

h m n r   h m n r

FAMILY 4
Letters with inverted arches:

u y   u y

FAMILY 5
Letters with the O counter shape:

a d g q   a d g q

FAMILY 6
Letters with inverted O shape:

b p   b p

FAMILY 7
Letters with elliptical curves:

o e c s   o e c s

FAMILY 8
Letters with horizontal crossbars:

f t   f t

9

CAPITAL FAMILIES

Capital letters are presented in family groups according to similar widths.

FAMILY I – WIDE

Width equals height: Width more than height:

C G D O Q   M W

FAMILY 2 – MEDIUM

Width equals 4/5 of height:

A H K N T U V X Y Z

FAMILY 3 – NARROW

Width equals 1/2 of height:

E F L · B P R S J · I

PARTS OF A LETTER

MONOLINE TOOL

EDGED PEN

SPACING

Generally two verticals have the most space between them.

hill
IN

A vertical and a curve are closer together.

home
ON

Two curves are closest.
(When writing in all caps, space them wider apart than when writing in caps & lower-case.)

look
DO

Leave about the width of lower-case n between words.

WRITING LINES

Three measurements for distance between lines of writing are included in this book. They include 10 mm, 7 mm, and 4 mm spaces.   (Lined practice sheets are included at the end of this book.)

Lines:

ASCENDER LINE (formal and chancery italic)

10mm   CAP LINE   and imaginary ascender line for basic and cursive italic

WAIST LINE

10 mm   imaginary branching line for lower-case

BASE LINE

10mm   imaginary descender line for basic and cursive italic

DESCENDER LINE (formal and chancery italic)

10 mm SPACE

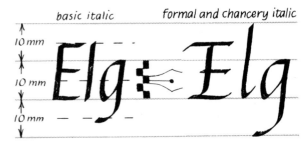

basic italic   formal and chancery italic

7 mm SPACE

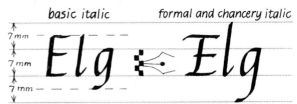

basic italic   formal and chancery italic

4 mm SPACE

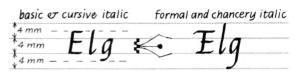

basic & cursive italic   formal and chancery italic

EVALUATING YOUR WORK

As you progress through this book, check your writing for the 7 characteristics of legibility.

I. SHAPE

Are you mastering the letter shapes as you trace & write? The italic lower-case letters are elliptical in nature.

CONSISTENT WITH MODEL · DIFFERENT FROM MODEL

shape shape

2. STROKE SEQUENCE

Are you memorizing the number and direction of the strokes of each letter?

Note:
The number of strokes of some letters changes when you switch from the monoline tool to the edged pen.

e.g. I stroke with mono-line tool — 2 strokes with edged pen

3. SIZE

Are the sizes of your letters in proper proportion to one another?

CONSISTENT WITH MODEL · DIFFERENT FROM MODEL

size size

The counter widths of most lower-case letters are 2 pen widths when using the edged pen.

4. SLOPE (letter slant)

Are you writing with a consistent letter slope? (Choose the slope that's comfortable for you, between 0° and 15°.)

|||| 0° |||| 5° //// 10° //// 15°

CONSISTENT LETTER SLOPE · IRREGULAR LETTER SLOPE

slope slope

5. SPACING WITHIN A WORD

Are you keeping your letters close together? Study the examples. Italic is tightly spaced.

CONSISTENT WITH MODEL · LETTERS TOO WIDELY SPACED

italic i t a l i c

6. SPACING BETWEEN WORDS

Are you leaving approximately the width of n between words?

These words are well spaced. Poorly spaced words.

7. SPEED

Is your speed consistent with your purpose?

SLOW DELIBERATE WRITING — very carefully written reports, business letters, thank you notes, applications, forms, maps, signs, term papers (...the writing in this book!)

MODERATE WRITING — more rapidly written letters and notes to friends, daily school assignments, drafts of poems, stories.

RAPID WRITING — very fast writing for note taking, jotting down ideas, phone messages, grocery lists.

WRITING HINTS

HOW TO SIT

For best results, rest your feet flat on the floor and keep your back comfortably straight. Rest your forearms on the writing surface. A flat surface is adequate for monoline tool writing (pencil, ballpoint, fibertip), but a slanted surface is more comfortable for both monoline and edged pen writing.

flat surface

slanted surface

Note:
For long periods of writing, prop up one foot to avoid back fatigue.

TOOL POSITION

Hold your monoline tool or edged pen with the thumb and index finger, resting it on the middle finger. Rest the shaft of the writing tool near the large knuckle. Hold your tool firmly, but avoid pinching. To relax your hand, tap index finger on tool 3 times. Repeat at intervals.

A comfortable hold will result in better writing!

PAPER POSITION
EDGED PEN WRITING · CHAPTERS II–VII and IX

If you are right-handed, keep your book or paper <u>vertical</u>. (See A.) This will allow the pen edge to form the proper thicks & thins as you form the letters.

If you are left-handed, experiment to determine the correct book or paper position. Begin with the book turned 90° clockwise. (See B.) This may be suitable to achieve the proper thicks and thins. If not, try other positions, turning book slightly counter clockwise each time. (See C.)

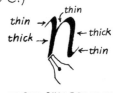

thin

thin → ← thick
thick → ← thin

EDGED PEN POSITION

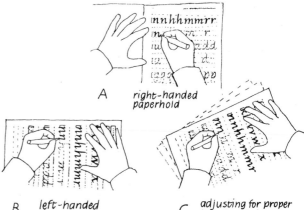

A   right-handed paperhold

B   left-handed paperhold

C   adjusting for proper left-handed hold

Position C also may be useful for the left-oblique nib.

PAPER POSITION FOR EDGED PEN

PEN EDGE ANGLE

The angle of your pen edge to the writing line (base line) determines where the thicks & thins occur.

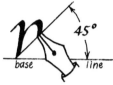

LOWER-CASE

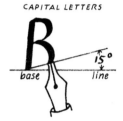

CAPITAL LETTERS

RIGHT-HANDED POSITION

If you are left-handed, hold your pen comfortably. Then experiment with various paper positions to achieve the proper thicks and thins.

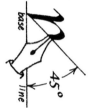

LOWER-CASE

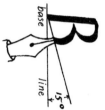

CAPITAL LETTERS

BEGINNING LEFT-HANDED POSITION

MATERIALS

WRITING TOOLS

MONOLINE TOOLS (Chapters II-V and VIII-X)

No. 2 pencil, medium or fine fiber-tip pen, or ballpoint.

In this book we used Flair pens and Le Pen by Marvy. For the small marginal notes we used the Koh-i-noor Rapidograph pens.

EDGED PENS (Chapters II-X)

Any fountain pens or dip nibs similar to the sizes shown below may be used to write in this book.

Edged dip pen nibs are used with an appropriate holder. They include: Brause, Mitchell, and Speedball by Hunt.

In this book, Brause nibs were used for Chapters I and X and all headings. Hunt's Speedball C-0 was used for pp. 104-105.

PENHOLDERS WITH DIP NIBS · FIBERTIP PENS

Many edged pens with fiber tips are available, among them: Eberhard Faber (Design Stripe Series), Hunt (Elegant Writer Series), Niji (Niji Stylist Series), and Pentalic (Lettering Markers).

Edged fountain pens include: Osmiroid, Parker, Platignum & Sheaffer.

For the majority of writing in this book, we used the Calligraphy NoNonsense fountain pen set by Sheaffer. The Sheaffer pen set contains one pen, three nibs (fine, medium, and broad), and ink cartridges.

COMPARISON OF PEN SIZES

FOUNTAIN PENS

Sheaffer	FINE (slightly less than 1 mm)	MEDIUM (slightly less than 1½ mm)	BROAD (approximately 2 mm)
Osmiroid	MEDIUM	B-2	B-3
Platignum	MEDIUM	B-2	B-3

DIP NIBS

Brause	1 mm	1½ mm	2 mm
Speedball	C-5	C-4	C-3

Left-handed nibs are available for some dip nibs and fountain pens. The left-handed nib has a left-oblique edge.

Note:
Dip nibs must be immersed in ink.
Fountain pens hold their own ink supply.

In addition to manufactured tools, others may be cut by hand – quills, reeds, ice cream sticks & tongue depressors.

(Use a very sharp utility knife or X-acto blade. A professional penknife is essential for cutting quills.)

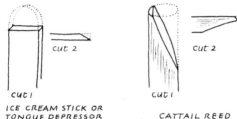

cut 2

cut 1

ICE CREAM STICK OR TONGUE DEPRESSOR

cut 2

cut 1

CATTAIL REED

(for large letters)

INKS

Be sure to use fountain pen ink in fountain pens. Some fountain pens come with ink cartridges; other pens require bottled ink. Some fountain pen inks are: Higgins Fountain Pen India, Higgins Sepia Calligraphy (brown), Parker Super Quink, Pelikan 4001, Pelikan Fount India, and Sheaffer Scrip. In addition to black, many colors are available.

Some dip pen inks are: Calli by Steig, Higgins Eternal Black, and Winsor & Newton. (Many inks may be used for both fountain and dip pens.)

Shake or stir both fountain pen and dip pen inks before using, and replace cap after use to avoid evaporation.

PAINTS

Transparent watercolors and gouache (opaque watercolors) may be used for color work in addition to colored inks. Use pan or tube paints with dip nibs only.

reservoir

Load brush with watercolor, then paint into dip pen reservoir.

PAPERS

For practice, white bond or duplicating paper usually provides a suitable writing surface. Avoid onionskin or easy-to-erase paper. The best way to select paper is to write on a sample of it. The paper should accept ink without feathering.

Both letters 1 & 2 were written with the same pen and ink on different paper.

¹*n* feathering→ ²*n*

Many high-quality text-weight handmade, mold-made, and machine-made papers are available. Some of them are: Bodleian, Charter Oak & Hayle (handmade); Michelangelo, Nideggen, Ingres & Rives (mold-made); and Gilbert Bond, Neenah Bond & Strathmore Bond (machine-made). Use cover stock when a heavier weight of paper is desired.

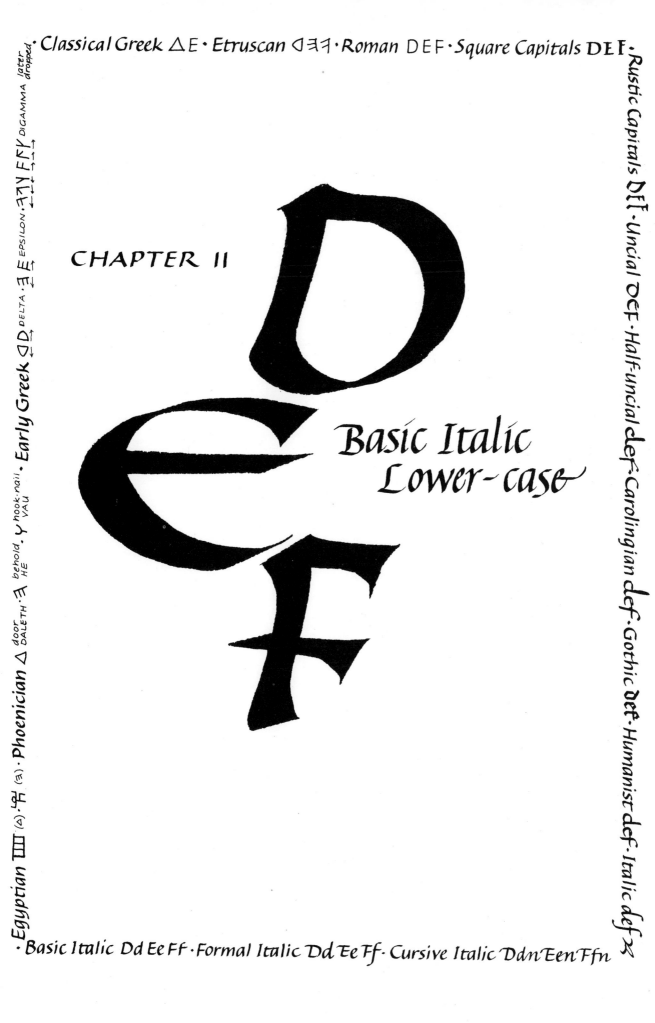

CHAPTER II

Basic Italic
Lower-case

BASIC ITALIC LOWER-CASE FAMILIES
FAMILY 1   2   3   4   5   6   7   8
i l j · k v w x z · n h m r · u y · a d g q · b p · o e c s · f t

For instructions about writing in this book see Chapter 1, page 8.

MONOLINE TOOL
10 mm body height

note height of ascender · · · · · · · · · · · · · · · ascender line
waist line
10mm body height
base line
note length of descender
descender line

FAMILY 1
i, l & j

touches at center
90° angle (like corner of page)
note axis of v shape same as slope -5°

FAMILY 2
k, v, w, x & z

crosses at center

branching out at center
note arch shape of counter

FAMILY 3
n, h, m & r

branching out at center
counters equal
each arch slightly narrower than counter of n

OR

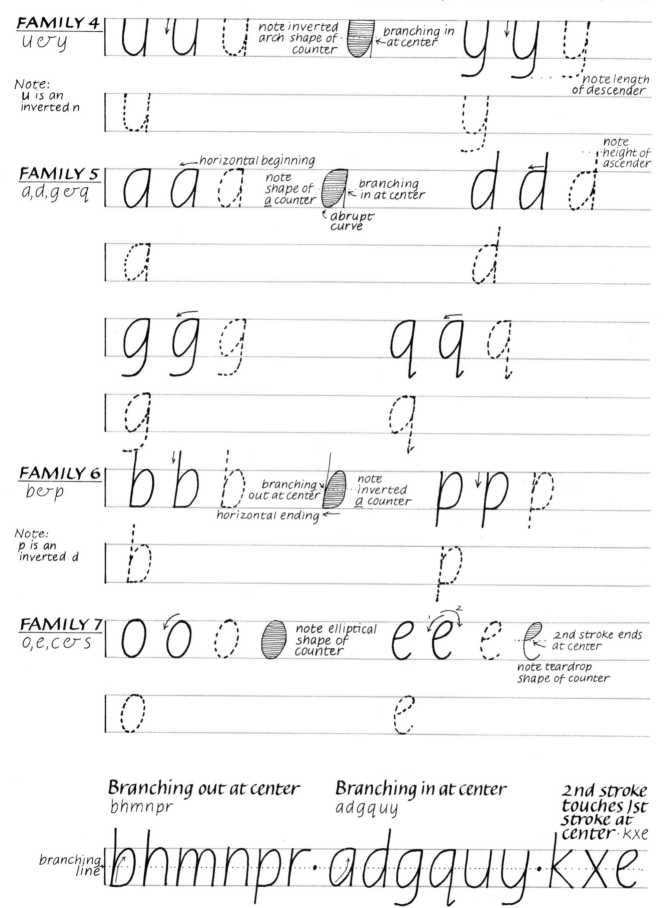

FAMILY 4
u & y

Note:
u is an
inverted n

note inverted
arch shape of
counter

branching in
at center

note length
of descender

FAMILY 5
a, d, g & q

horizontal beginning

note
shape of
a counter

branching
in at center

abrupt
curve

note
height of
ascender

FAMILY 6
b & p

Note:
p is an
inverted d

branching
out at center

note
inverted
a counter

horizontal ending

FAMILY 7
o, e, c & s

note elliptical
shape of
counter

2nd stroke ends
at center

note teardrop
shape of counter

Branching out at center
bhmnpr

Branching in at center
adgquy

2nd stroke
touches 1st
stroke at
center · kxe

branching
line

bhmnpr · adgquy · kxe

17

horizontal beginning of c & s

note straight diagonal

horizontal ending

FAMILY 7 (continued)

Note crossbar of f & t begins slightly to the left of the downstroke.

FAMILY 8
f & t

Crossbar lines up with top of f and bottom of t.

SLOPE 5°

WIDTH OF LETTERS
Use n as the basis of the Width for all letters except i, l, m & w. (Note r is slightly narrower than n.)

FAMILIES 1-8
with branching, ascender, and descender lines

abcdefghjknpq
rstuvwxyz · l · m · w

ilj · kvwxz · nhmr · uy

adgq · bp · oecs · ft

ASCENDERS
bdfhkl · gjpqy · t   *slight ascender*

DESCENDERS
p

SPACING
3 rules for even spacing of letters in words

1. Two verticals farthest apart
hill h
counter *interspace*
The width of the interspace is always less than the width of the counter of a letter.

2. A vertical and a curve closer
home h

3. Two curves closest
pod p

PANGRAM
A sentence containing every letter of the alphabet

a quick brown fox

Note: Keep width of an n between words.
a

jumps over the

j

The word lower-case is a term from printing. The small letters or minuscules (pieces of type) were kept in the lower case (lower drawer). The large letters, capitals or majuscules, were kept in the upper case.

lazy dog

i

19

ilj · kvwxz · nhmr · uy ·

i

waist
line
7mm
base
line

The letters are
written in a
7 mm space.

adgq · bp · oecs · ft ·

a

The earliest form of writ-

Trace the model
letters and
words, then
write them in
the space below.

T

ing was pictographic. The

i

writer conveyed ideas by

Keep space of
an _n_ between
words.

W

means of pictures, such as

CAVE PAINTING
Bison
Magdalenian
period
Niaux, France

m

the Paleolithic

t

cave paintings.

c

CAVE TO RENAISSANCE by Benjamin Rowland, Jr.
(Shorewood Publishers, 1965). Reproduced by permission.

MONOLINE TOOL

The letters are now written in a 4 mm space.

Trace the model words, then write in the space below.

Do keep ascenders and descenders one half of the body height.

a d g ←ascender ←descender

Capital letters are the height of ascenders.
(More on capitals in Chapter III.)

It is generally accepted that the most

ancient system of writing was developed

by the Sumerians of Mesopotamia.

They were an industrious people who

developed an economy based on farming

and were the original keepers of records.

Initially the Sumerians wrote with sharp

SUMERIAN PICTOGRAMS AND IDEOGRAMS

PICTOGRAMS
stylized symbols of pictures

	EARLY	LATER POSITION	EARLY CUNEIFORM
ox			
bird			

IDEOGRAMS
symbols for ideas

stand
go

sun
day
time

Note:
Before 4000 B.C. settlers from the north came to Mesopotamia, but it may be that the Sumerians did not inhabit the region until nearly 3000 B.C.

tools on stone,

metal, and clay. At

first they used

symbols now called

pictograms. Later

they devised symbols that represented ideas —

ideograms.

Write words of your choice on this line.

21

LOWER-CASE FAMILIES written with the edged pen.
The edged pen enhances the letterforms because of the contrast of thicks and thins formed by the chisel edge.

BROAD NIB
2 mm
(Refer to p. 13 for chart of pen sizes used in this book.)

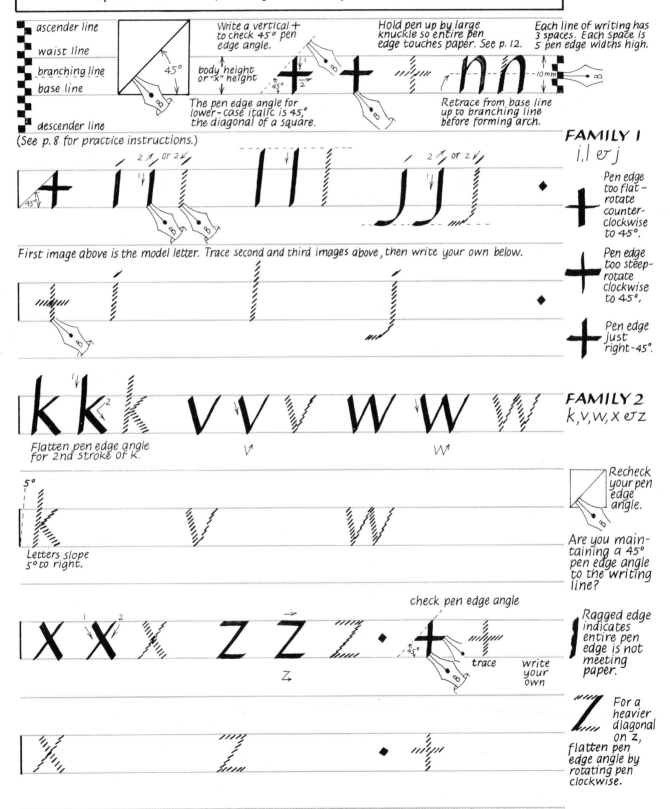

ascender line
waist line
branching line
base line
descender line

Write a vertical + to check 45° pen edge angle.

body height or "x" height

The pen edge angle for lower-case italic is 45°, the diagonal of a square.

Hold pen up by large knuckle so entire pen edge touches paper. See p. 12.

Retrace from base line up to branching line before forming arch.

Each line of writing has 3 spaces. Each space is 5 pen edge widths high.

10mm

(See p. 8 for practice instructions.)

FAMILY 1
i, l & j

2↗ or 2↙

First image above is the model letter. Trace second and third images above, then write your own below.

Pen edge too flat - rotate counter-clockwise to 45°.

Pen edge too steep - rotate clockwise to 45°.

Pen edge just right - 45°.

FAMILY 2
k, v, w, x & z

Flatten pen edge angle for 2nd stroke of k.

Letters slope 5° to right.

Recheck your pen edge angle.

Are you maintaining a 45° pen edge angle to the writing line?

check pen edge angle

trace   write your own

Ragged edge indicates entire pen edge is not meeting paper.

For a heavier diagonal on z, flatten pen edge angle by rotating pen clockwise.

BROAD NIB *First image below is the model letter. Trace the second and third images. On the following line write your own letters.*

FAMILY 3
n, h, m & r

All letters in families 3 and 4 are 1 stroke letters. Don't lift pen until you've completed each letter.

Retrace these letters from base to branching line before branching away to form arch.

5° letter slope

FAMILY 4
u & y

To check letter widths: flatten pen to horizontal, then establish 2 pen widths in the counters of n, h, u, y, a, d, g, q, b, p, and o.

Keep the arm of r short.

FAMILY 5
a, d, g & q

This the basic shape of family 5:

branching line

Complete basic

o

shape before completing a, d, g, & q.

Do touch the guide lines as you write.

FAMILY 6
b & p

Note:
Second stroke
begins at
base line.

◆

Note:
Trace all mod-
els with ink
of a color
other than
black so you
can tell if
you deviate
from the
given lines.

◆

FAMILY 7
o, e, c & s

overlap
second
stroke

overlap
second
stroke

C Begin c
horizon-
tally
hanging from
waist line.

S When
writing
s, flatten
pen edge angle –
pull elbow to
body if right-
handed, or push
left elbow away
from body if
left-handed.

or

FAMILY 8
f & t

l When using
first direc-
tional stroke
sequence for t,
the first stroke
has a serif.
Begin stroke l
slightly less
than l pen
width below
waist line, ex-
tend l pen
width above
waist line.

Note:
Leave approximately 2 pen edge widths within the counters of
h, n, u, y, a, d, g, q, b, p, and o for proper letter widths.
Measure at branching line.

branching
line

Write n, d, and o above,
then measure counters with
a 0° pen edge angle.

**NOTES
ON
SPACING**

Two down-strokes have the most room between them.	**▯·hill**	A down-stroke and a curve are a bit closer	**▯·lot**	Two curves almost touch.	**▯·look**

**PUNCTU-
ATION** — The question mark & exclamation point are written at cap height, (7½ pen edge widths, or halfway between the waist line & ascender line).

**BROAD NIB
PANGRAM**

 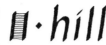 Why did Max become

Note:
See p. 36 for capital letters.

Note:
Use a dot or a jot over lower-case i and j.

dot→**i̇** jot→**j̇**

eloquent over a zany

Leave approximately the width of n between words.

ft—write two downstrokes, **ft** then cross them together.

gift like jodhpurs?

Note:
Crossbar on f and t extends slightly to left of horizontal bar to form ◢.

Cuneiform, developed by the

MEDIUM NIB
slightly less than 1½ mm

Sumerians, was written on clay

This page is written with a medium nib, slightly less than 1½ mm.

tablets with a wedge-shaped

Check your pen edge angle by tracing over the + and n:

stylus made of

+

n

The + is written vertically. The n slopes approximately 5° to the right.

reed, wood, bone,

Reminder: Leave about the width of n between words.

to be

or metal.

The hyphen is a short horizontal line that sits on the branching line.

e-s

This system flourished

You may join f and l as shown.

for over two thousand years.

CUNEIFORM *Sumerian medical tablet, ca. 2100 B.C. (The University Museum, University of Pennsylvania) Reproduced by permission.*

Because it was difficult to draw curves & circles in clay, the Sumerians eventually designed a wedge-shaped writing tool for increased legibility & speed.

FINE NIB
slightly less than 1mm

Egyptian writing originated in about

3000 B.C. — a period of strong Sumerian

The idea of Sumerian dominance supports the argument that Egyptian writing was based on the Sumerian forms.

influence. The Sumerians and the

Egyptians went through similar stages —

pictogram, ideogram, and phonogram – but

The Egyptian syllabary, the phonetic part of the language, consisted of about 80 signs with 2 consonants plus vowels in addition to the 24 signs.

the Egyptians also created a system of

24 hieroglyphic alphabetical signs.

Three types

Illustration:
HIEROGLYPHIC
SCRIPT
Portion of the
Lion-hunt Scarab
of Amenophis III,
18th Dynasty.
(The Portland Art
Museum, Portland,
Oregon) Reproduced
by permission.

of scripts

were used in

ancient Egypt:

hieroglyphic, hieratic, and demotic.

Quotation marks hang at cap height.

"Hieroglyphic" was derived from Greek

words meaning "sacred inscriptions" and

was writing carved in stone. Two cursive

| w

styles, hieratic and demotic, were written

| s

with a pen.

| w

The hieratic

| T

HIERATIC SCRIPT (British Museum)
Reproduced by courtesy of the Trustees of the British Museum.

script was

| s

directly

| d

DEMOTIC SCRIPT (British Museum)
Reproduced by courtesy of the Trustees of the British Museum.

derived from the carved forms. The demotic

| d

script, a less pictorial form, was a short-

| s

hand version of hieratic.

| h

       Two great inventions of the Egyptians

| T

shaped the history of writing: papyrus, a

| s

writing surface formed from papyrus

| w

reeds, and the reed brush-pen cut from

| r

the same plant.

| t

Note:
This page is ruled with only a base line for practice. Begin to feel the proper height by tracing the models, then write them below.

The writing in both examples is from left to right on papyrus.

We read lower-case letters by interpreting the shapes of the tops of the letters:

handwriting

For that reason, keep the shape and height of your letterforms consistent.

Paper:
from the Latin papūrus, the aquatic reed of the Nile and the paperlike material made from it. The name came also to mean paper made of cotton and other fiber.

CHAPTER III

Basic
Italic
Capitals

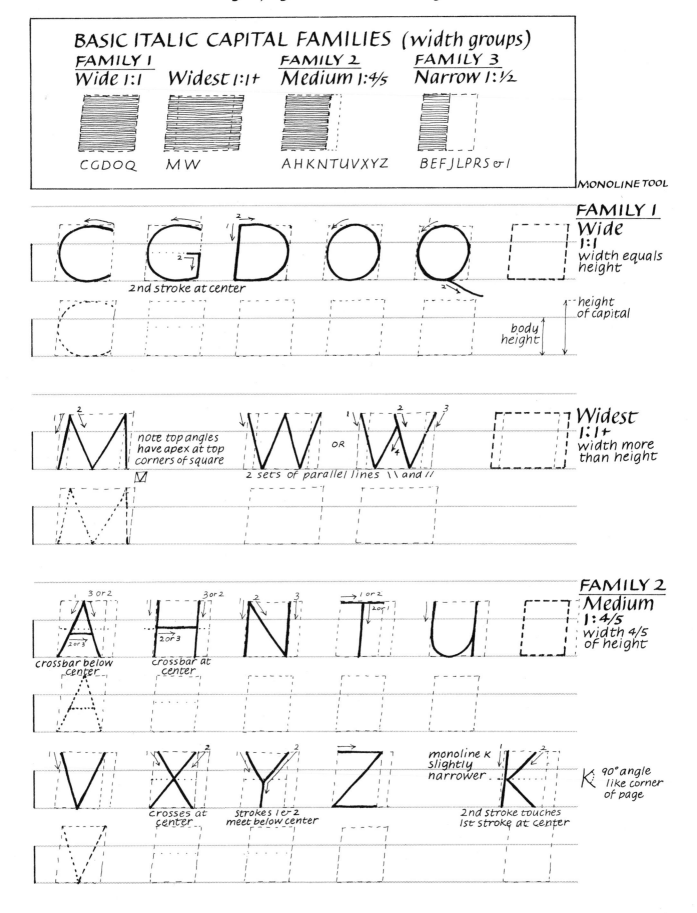

BASIC ITALIC CAPITAL FAMILIES (width groups)

FAMILY 1
Wide 1:1   Widest 1:1+

FAMILY 2
Medium 1:4/5

FAMILY 3
Narrow 1:½

CGDOQ   MW   AHKNTUVXYZ   BEFJLPRS & I

MONOLINE TOOL

FAMILY 1
Wide
1:1
width equals
height

2nd stroke at center

height
of capital

body
height

**Widest
1:1+
width more
than height**

note top angles
have apex at top
corners of square

2 sets of parallel lines \\ and //

**FAMILY 2
Medium
1:4/5
width 4/5
of height**

3 or 2   3 or 2   2 3   1 or 2   2 or 1

crossbar below
center

crossbar at
center

2 or 3   2 or 3

monoline K
slightly
narrower

K 90° angle
like corner
of page

crosses at
center

strokes 1 & 2
meet below center

2nd stroke touches
1st stroke at center

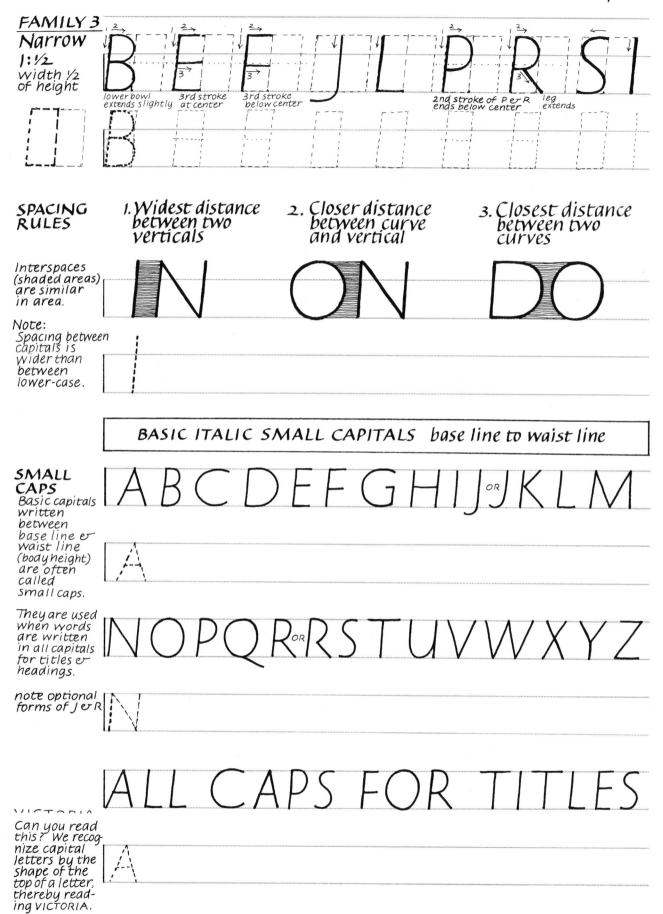

**FAMILY 3
Narrow
1:½**
width ½
of height

B E F J L P R S I

B

lower bowl extends slightly · 3rd stroke at center · 3rd stroke below center · 2nd stroke of P or R ends below center · leg extends

**SPACING
RULES**

1. Widest distance between two verticals
2. Closer distance between curve and vertical
3. Closest distance between two curves

Interspaces (shaded areas) are similar in area.

IN   ON   DO

Note:
Spacing between capitals is wider than between lower-case.

I

BASIC ITALIC SMALL CAPITALS base line to waist line

**SMALL
CAPS**
Basic capitals written between base line & waist line (body height) are often called small caps.

ABCDEFGHIJ or JKLM

A

They are used when words are written in all capitals for titles & headings.

NOPQR or RSTUVWXYZ

note optional forms of J & R

N

ALL CAPS FOR TITLES

VICTORIA

Can you read this? We recognize capital letters by the shape of the top of a letter, thereby reading VICTORIA.

A

BASIC ITALIC CAPITALS AND LOWER-CASE

Capital height is 1½ times body height.

Height of capital and ascender is the same.

10mm

Note: Center of capital falls just below waist line.

7mm

Note:
Be aware of
center of
capital.

Ligatures are
the characters
formed by the
connecting of
two or more
letters into a
single form.
Basic italic
Capitals may
share a com-
mon down-
stroke for
convenience
or decorative
effect.

THE
NEW
HUE
THANKS

Basic italic
lower-case
letters may
also form
ligatures for
convenience,
such as, tt &
ff. When
connecting
with the cross-
bar of t, short-
en the bottom
curve of t
slightly.

tt ff
ti tr tu ty
fi fr fu fy

Aa Bb Cc Dd Ee Ff Gg Hh Ii ↕4mm

Jj Kk Ll Mm Nn Oo Pp Qq Rr

Ss Tt Uu Vv Ww Xx Yy Zz

The Phoenicians were the inventors of our alphabet. Berthold Ullman, in ANCIENT WRITING AND ITS INFLUENCE, notes that the Semites used the acrophonic principle. The picture of an object came to be used as a representation for the initial letter of the word for that object.

EGYPTIAN HIEROGLYPH		SEMITIC LETTER (PHOENICIAN)	SEMITIC WORD
house 	☐ or ☐ came to represent	 ⊴	first letter of BETH (house)
door 	⊞ (temple door?) came to represent	 △ (door flap of tent?)	first letter of DALETH (door)
water 	∧∧∧ came to represent	 W	first letter of MEM (water)
human head 	𓁶 came to represent	 ⊴	first letter of RESH (head)

The Phoenician alphabet of
22 symbols had only consonants.

The direction of writing was

from right to left, as it continues

in Hebrew today.

The Greek alphabet was based on the

shapes and names of Phoenician symbols.

The earliest Greek writing was also from

right to left. A transitional mode of writing

followed. It was called BOUSTROPHEDON, "OX-

turning": one line from left to right, the next

from right to left. The letters also changed

direction.

PHOENICIAN
Adapted from
Inscription
9th century B.C.
(Musée du Louvre,
Paris)

PHOENICIAN
△ 𝟄
aleph beth

GREEK (EARLY)
A 𝟄
alpha beta

BOUS (ox)
STREPHEIN
(to turn)
"ox-turning",
as the fields
are plowed
by oxen

ABΓDEFBIKLMΜ OΓO →
Q?OYM⅃℣IB℩∃ᗡↃᙠA ←

EARLY GREEK
Lemnos Stella
(side view)
Athens
6th century B.C.
(National Archaeo-
logical Museum,
Athens)
Reproduced
by permission.

35

BASIC ITALIC CAPITAL FAMILIES · EDGED PEN

(Refer to p.13 for chart of pen sizes used in this book.)

Pen edge angle 15° for capitals (a flatter angle than the 45° for lower-case)

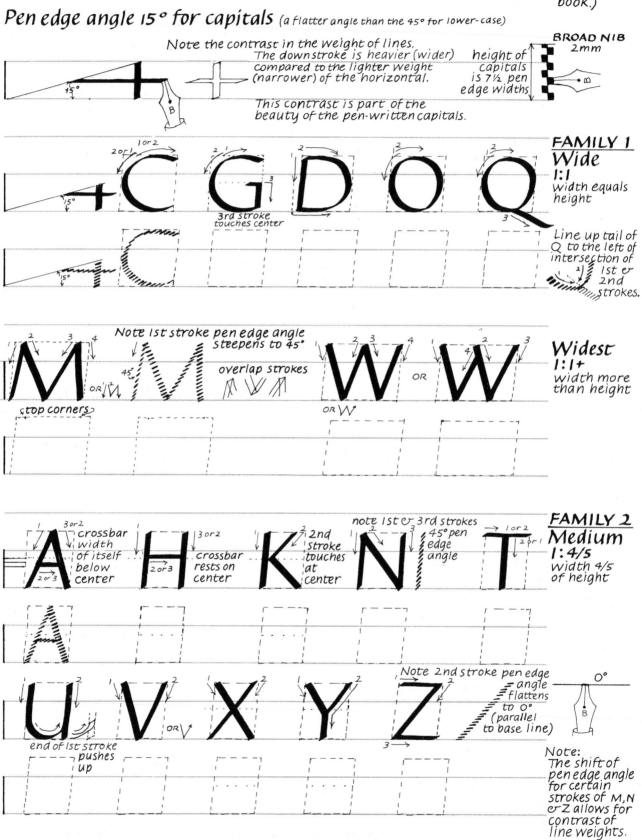

Note the contrast in the weight of lines. The downstroke is heavier (wider) compared to the lighter weight (narrower) of the horizontal.

This contrast is part of the beauty of the pen-written capitals.

height of capitals is 7½ pen edge widths

BROAD NIB 2mm

FAMILY 1
Wide
1:1
width equals height

3rd stroke touches center

Line up tail of Q to the left of intersection of 1st & 2nd strokes.

Note 1st stroke pen edge angle steepens to 45°

overlap strokes

stop corners

Widest
1:1+
width more than height

FAMILY 2
Medium
1:4/5
width 4/5 of height

crossbar width of itself below center

crossbar rests on center

2nd stroke touches at center

note 1st & 3rd strokes 45° pen edge angle

Note 2nd stroke pen edge angle flattens to 0° (parallel to base line)

end of 1st stroke pushes up

Note: The shift of pen edge angle for certain strokes of M,N & Z allows for contrast of line weights.

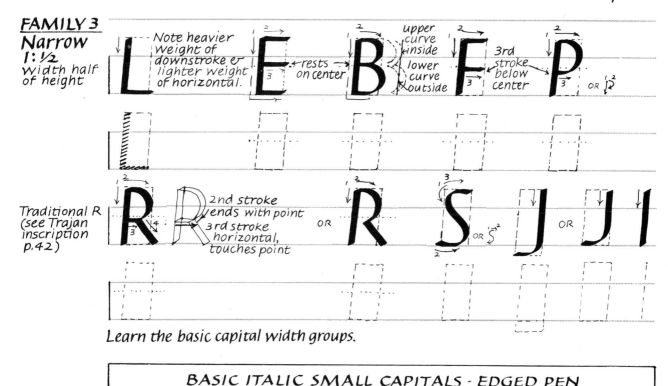

FAMILY 3
Narrow
1 : ½
Width half
of height

Note heavier weight of downstroke & lighter weight of horizontal.

rests on center

upper curve inside
lower curve outside

3rd stroke below center

OR

Traditional R
(see Trajan
inscription
p.42)

2nd stroke ends with point
3rd stroke horizontal, touches point

OR

OR

Learn the basic capital width groups.

BASIC ITALIC SMALL CAPITALS · EDGED PEN

SMALL CAPS
Remain at 15° pen edge angle and maintain same letter width groups. These are basic caps written at 5 pen edge widths.

Use basic small caps for titles, headings, posters, banners, addresses & certificates.

ABCDEFGHIJJKLM

NOPQRRSTUVWXYZ

MIXED CAPS
Basic and small caps may be used separately or together.

MIXED CAPITALS

BASIC ITALIC CAPITALS AND LOWER-CASE

Capitals are written with a pen edge angle of 15°

Shift back to a pen edge angle of 45° for lower-case.

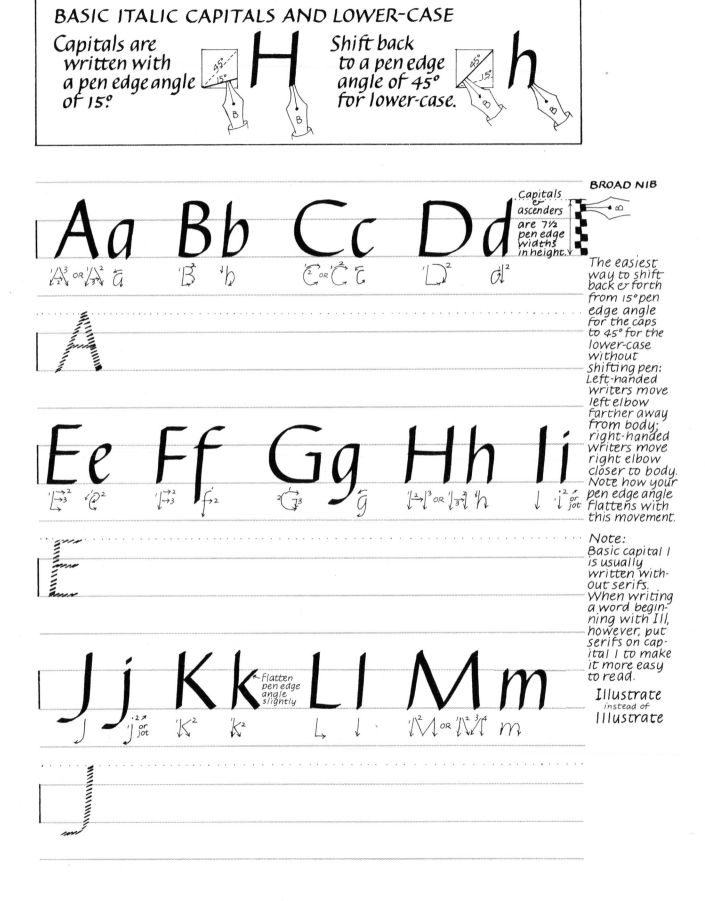

BROAD NIB

Capitals & ascenders are 7½ pen edge widths in height.

The easiest way to shift back & forth from 15° pen edge angle for the caps to 45° for the lower-case without shifting pen: Left-handed writers move left elbow farther away from body; right-handed writers move right elbow closer to body. Note how your pen edge angle flattens with this movement.

Note: Basic capital I is usually written without serifs. When writing a word beginning with Ill, however, put serifs on capital I to make it more easy to read.

Illustrate
instead of
Illustrate

flatten pen edge angle slightly

Reminder:
Lower-case t
starts slightly
below waist
line.

Extend only
1 pen edge
width above
waist line to
avoid white

AVOID

OR
begin t
1 pen
edge
angle
above waist line

Push back up
on first up-
stroke so that
second down-
stroke over-
laps—both on
the capital &
lower-case w.

NOTE:

Cap & ascender height
(1½ times body height)

waist line

base line

body
height

descender length

If preferred, write
basic italic lower-
case with taller
ascenders and
longer descenders
for a more formal
appearance.

Practice these
letters again
using a guide
sheet (pages
126-28).

MEDIUM NIB

After the 5th century B.C.

A

the direction of most Greek

l

In the Classical Greek inscription from the 1st century B.C., shown below, the writing goes from left to right.

writing was from left

W

ΣΙΤΑΦΗΝΝ ΕΛΝΟΜ
ΚΕΛΕΠΓ ΤΕ ΜΔΝ ΔΙΕΓ
ΔΙΚΛΣΤΩΝ ΚΑΛΩΤΙΝΛ
ΒΟΜ ΘΗΙΓΟΝΤΑ ΔΝΛ
ΒΗΟΙΛΛΩΙΟΓΟΦΙΝ
ΚΔΙΟΓΝΕΠΓΕΟΠΓΟΧΛ
ΚΕΛΕΓΟΓΛΙΝΟΙΔ ΚΑ

to right. The Greeks

e

GREEK SCRIPT *Oration of Hyperides, 1st century B.C.*

(The British Library) *Reproduced by permission.*

added vowels to the alphabet-

a

a major contribution.

a

ETRUSCAN ALPHABET *The Marsiliana Abecedarium, an 8th century B.C. writing tablet.*

(Museo Archeologico, Florence) *Reproduced by permission.*

The Etruscans acquired

T

the alphabet from the Greeks.

e

The Etruscans were the dominant culture in Italy 1000-509 B.C. They remain a people of mystery, as no one to this date has been able to translate their writings.

FINE NIB

· ROMAN LETTERS ·

Basic and small caps used for heading.

The historical importance of the

Remember to flatten pen edge angle for s and for horizontal crossbar of f and t.

Etruscans lies in their influence on early

Rome.

The alphabet passed from the Greeks

via the Etruscans to the Romans. By the

Note: Small caps used for "B.C."

3rd century B.C. the Latin alphabet attained

EARLY ROMAN CAPITALS Votive inscription, 2nd century B.C. (Biblioteca Apostolica Vaticana, Vatican City) Reproduced by permission.

Primitive serifs on the endings of many letters. Note first v.

a somewhat

consistent

pattern of

letterforms.

The early Roman inscriptions were

roughly formed monoline letters, but the

beginnings of serifs appeared about 200 B.C.

The Roman art of cutting letters in stone   *FINE NIB*

reached its peak in the 2nd century A.D.

Generally the letters were initially written

with a brush, incised in

stone or metal, then

painted.

These classical let-

terforms reappear at

various later periods in the history of

writing, reaching a high level of design

during the Renaissance.

The Roman incised capitals serve as

the basis of our written letters today.

SENATVSPOPV
IMP·CAESARI·DIV
TRAIANO·AVG·G
MAXIMOTRIBPO
ADDECLARANDVM

CLASSICAL ROMAN CAPITALS *Trajan Inscription, A.D. 114*
(Trajan Column, Roman Forum, Rome)

THE ROMAN LETTER by James Hayes (The Lakeside Press, R.R. Donnelley & Sons Company). Reproduced by permission.

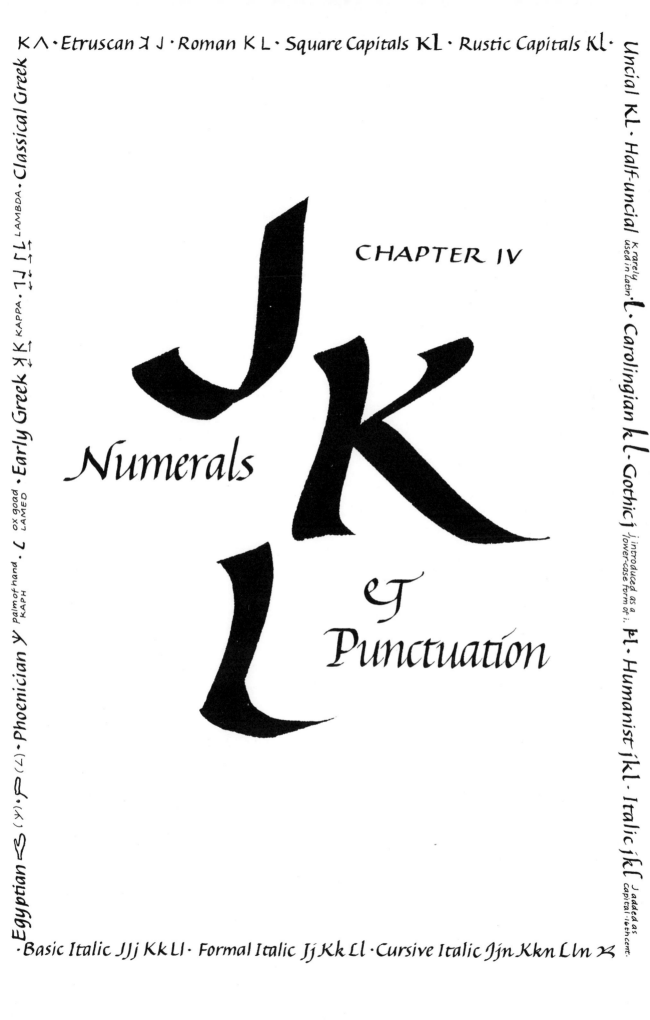

Classical Greek

Κ L LAMBDA · →

KAPPA ↓ K · →

Early Greek Ϟ ↓ →

ox goad L LAMED ·

Phoenician ϟ KAPH palm of hand ·

Egyptian ⟅⟆ (ϟ) ⌐ (L) ·

CHAPTER IV

Numerals

K

J

L

&

Punctuation

Uncial KL · Half-uncial K rarely used in Latin L · Carolingian k l · Gothic j J introduced as a lower-case form of i · KL · Humanist jkl · Italic jkl J added as capital-16th cent.

NUMERALS

The word NUMBER stands for an idea—how many objects in a group. The word NUMERAL describes the symbol we use for the number idea.

CONTEMPORARY NUMERALS

MONOLINE TOOL

Trace each numeral, then write below.

Note:
2 is a full curve with a horizontal. The curve is the shape of half a Valentine heart: ♡

4—horizontal is wide

7— 7

SMALL NUMERALS
from waist line to base line

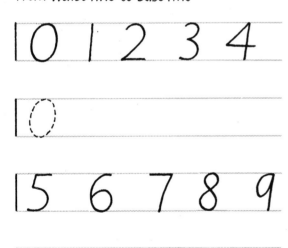

Note:

Are your numerals all the same height?

When writing small numerals are you touching both the waist and base lines?

HINDU-ARABIC NUMERALS

About 300 B.C. the Hindus of India were using a numeral system based on 10. They had a symbol for each number from 1 to 9 and a name for each power of 10. They would write "1 sata, 3 dasan, 8" as we would write 138.

About A.D. 600 the Hindus invented the zero, meaning "empty," which simplified their system.

During the 8th century A.D. the Arabs learned the Hindu system and assisted its spread to Europe 300 years later. However, the Hindu-Arabic system did not enjoy widespread use until the 1500s.

Small numerals: Use same stroke sequence as for larger ones.

6— Form an ellipse for the left counter-clockwise curve. Close the 6 with a circle.

9—alternate 9 Form partial circle from top, curving left counter-clockwise. Second stroke: form partial ellipse clockwise. Don't let it turn into g!

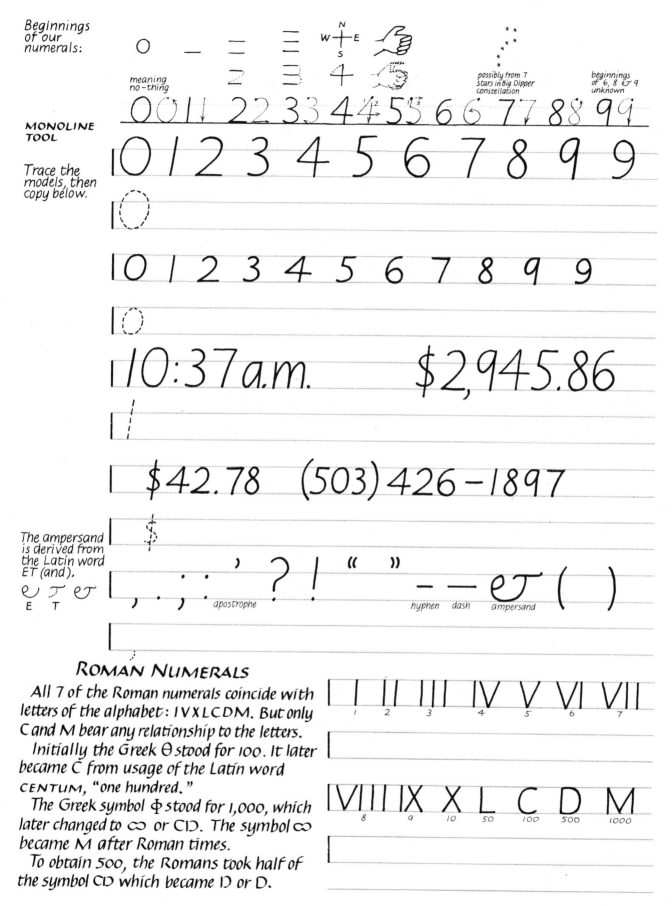

Beginnings of our numerals:

meaning no-thing

possibly from 7 Stars in Big Dipper Constellation

beginnings of 6, 8 & 9 unknown

MONOLINE TOOL

Trace the models, then copy below.

10:37 a.m. $2,945.86

$42.78   (503) 426-1897

The ampersand is derived from the Latin word ET (and).

E T

, . ; : ? ! " " – — & ( )

apostrophe   hyphen dash ampersand

ROMAN NUMERALS

All 7 of the Roman numerals coincide with letters of the alphabet: I V X L C D M. But only C and M bear any relationship to the letters.

Initially the Greek Θ stood for 100. It later became C from usage of the Latin word CENTUM, "one hundred."

The Greek symbol Φ stood for 1,000, which later changed to ∞ or CIƆ. The symbol ∞ became M after Roman times.

To obtain 500, the Romans took half of the symbol CIƆ which became IƆ or D.

I	II	III	IV	V	VI	VII
1	2	3	4	5	6	7

VIII	IX	X	L	C	D	M
8	9	10	50	100	500	1000

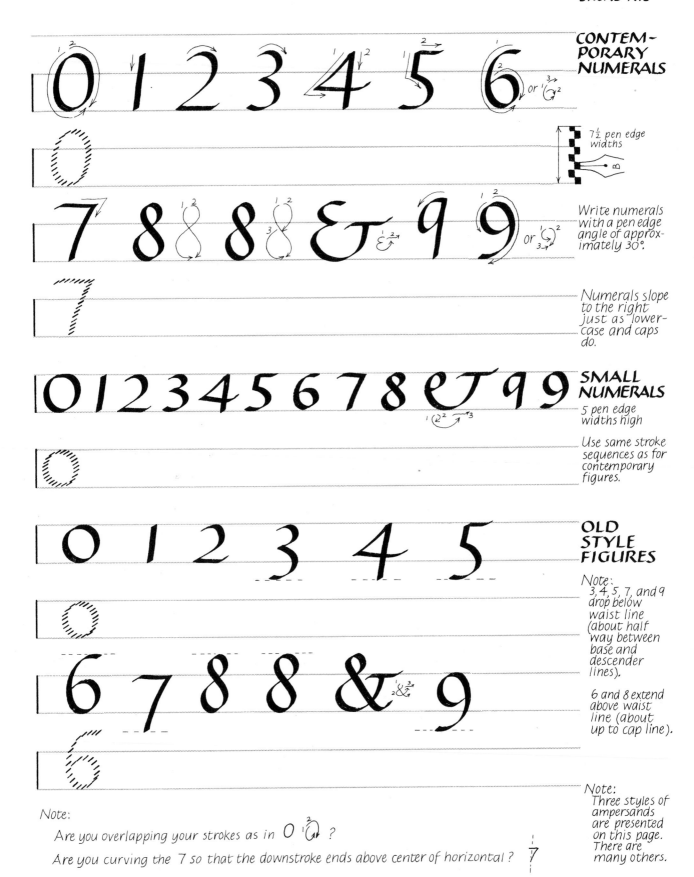

**CONTEM-
PORARY
NUMERALS**

$7\frac{1}{2}$ pen edge widths

Write numerals with a pen edge angle of approximately 30°.

Numerals slope to the right just as lower-case and caps do.

**SMALL
NUMERALS**

5 pen edge widths high

Use same stroke sequences as for contemporary figures.

**OLD
STYLE
FIGURES**

Note:
3, 4, 5, 7, and 9 drop below waist line (about half way between base and descender lines).

6 and 8 extend above waist line (about up to cap line).

Note:
Three styles of ampersands are presented on this page. There are many others.

Note:

Are you overlapping your strokes as in O ?

Are you curving the 7 so that the downstroke ends above center of horizontal ?

MEDIUM NIB

CONTEMPORARY NUMERALS

0 1 2 3 4 5 6 7 8 9 9

7½ pen edge widths high

O

SMALL NUMERALS

0 1 2 3 4 5 6 7 8 & 9 9

5 pen edge widths high

O

OLD STYLE FIGURES

0 1 2 3 4 5 6 7 8 & 9

O

PUNCTUATION

, . ; : ' ? ! " " -- & ( )

&

Address using old style figures.

Note: Small caps used for state.

7603 N.W. 158th Ave. Portland, OR 97264

ROMAN NUMERALS

I II III IV V VI VII VIII IX

1 2 3 4 5 6 7 8 9

X XI XII XX L C D M

10 11 12 20 50 100 500 1000

Can you decipher this? MCMLXXXVII _____

The Roman numeral system was the most widely used form of writing numbers until the late 1500s, when the Hindu-Arabic system became popular. One disadvantage of the Roman system: no symbol for zero!

The

The Hindu-Arabic system we use probably reached us via Arabia from a starting point in India. It arrived in Europe via Spain and developed into the system commonly used today.

The

FINE NIB

Paragraph practice using basic italic.

Trace the model words, then write the paragraph in the space provided.

0 1 2 3 4 5 6 7 8 9 · 0 1 2 3 4 5 6 7 8 9

REVIEW OF NUMERALS

0

0 1 2 3 4 5 6 7 8 9

0

THE AMPERSAND

One ideogram that has survived 2000 years is the ampersand, the sign &. It was invented by Cicero's freed slave Tiro in the 1st century B.C. and is still used today in several hundred languages.

The word "ampersand" derived from the sign sometimes being placed at the end of the alphabet. After reciting "...w, x, y, z," the speaker added "and, per se, and," meaning "and, by itself, and." Eventually the words "and," "per se," "and" became "ampersand."

AMPERSANDS

Through the ages, scribes have varied the design of the ampersand. The practice continues today. At left are four ampersands designed from the letters E and T.

48

CHAPTER V

Formal
Italic
Lower-case

FORMAL ITALIC LOWER-CASE

Serifs added to basic italic lower-case letters (Chapter II)
and ascenders and descenders lengthened

a becomes **a**   r becomes **r**   b becomes **b**   g becomes **g**

exit serif added   entrance serif added   ascender lengthened   descender lengthened

only k changes shape k becomes **k**

2 strokes   1 stroke

MONOLINE TOOL

ENTRANCE SERIF
slightly rounded angle

entrance serif added   exit serif added   entrance and exit serifs added   jot added

r r   a a   i i   m m   n n

EXIT SERIF
slightly rounded angle

slight ending serif on v & w   serifs on 2nd stroke of x are horizontal

u u   v v   w w   x x   z z   z

serifs on diagonal

ascender lengthened   ascender lengthened and exit serif added   ascender & descender lengthened

ASCENDERS
Letters with ascenders twice body height.

b b   d d   h h   k k   l l   f f

with edged pen use 2 strokes   k becomes 1 stroke

descender lengthened   entrance serif added and descender lengthened   jot added

DESCENDERS
Letters with descenders twice body height.

g g g g   j j   sharp serif   j j   sharp serif slightly higher   p p   roll over serif   y y

with edged pen use 2 strokes

with edged pen use 2 strokes   no change

o o   c c   e e   s s   t t

overlap strokes

FORMAL ITALIC LOWER-CASE · *Families 1–8*

Pen edge angle 45° for lower-case

BROAD NIB

45° angle is the diagonal of a square

Note:
Width of vertical line is equal to width of horizontal line.

equal width

FAMILY 1
i, l & j

ascender line

waist line

FAMILY 2
k, v, w, x & z

base line

descender line

branching at center

Note:
Pen edge angle may be flattened slightly for z.

crosses at center

FAMILY 3
n, h, m & r

Note:
Counter is two pen edge widths.

branching at center

FAMILY 4
u ʊ y

FAMILY 5
a, d, g ʊ q

NOTE:
two pen
edge
widths
at center

FAMILY 6
b ʊ p

ELLIPTICAL
CURVE on right
farthest
point
above
center
bpo

on left
farthest
point below
center
adgqceo

FAMILY 7
o, e, c ʊ s

slightly flatten pen
edge angle for s

SECOND STROKE
OF E
1. Curve to
   diagonal
2. short hori-
   zontal end

tear
drop
counter

FAMILY 8
f & t

slightly flatten pen edge angle for crossbar of f & t

OR

OR

SLOPE 5°

NOTE WIDTH
Most letters are the same width as n.

(m & w are wider i & l are narrower)

n a b c d e f g h j k

n o p q r s t u v x y z

PANGRAM
Note: f & t can share common crossbar

two verticals farthest apart

curve and a vertical closer

quick wafting zeph-

Note: Keep width of an n between words.

COSMIC FLOWER
(Lloyd Reynolds' name for fleur-de-lis)

two curves closest

yrs vex bold jim

CHECK:
① pen edge angle
② consistent slope
③ width of counter
④ branching line

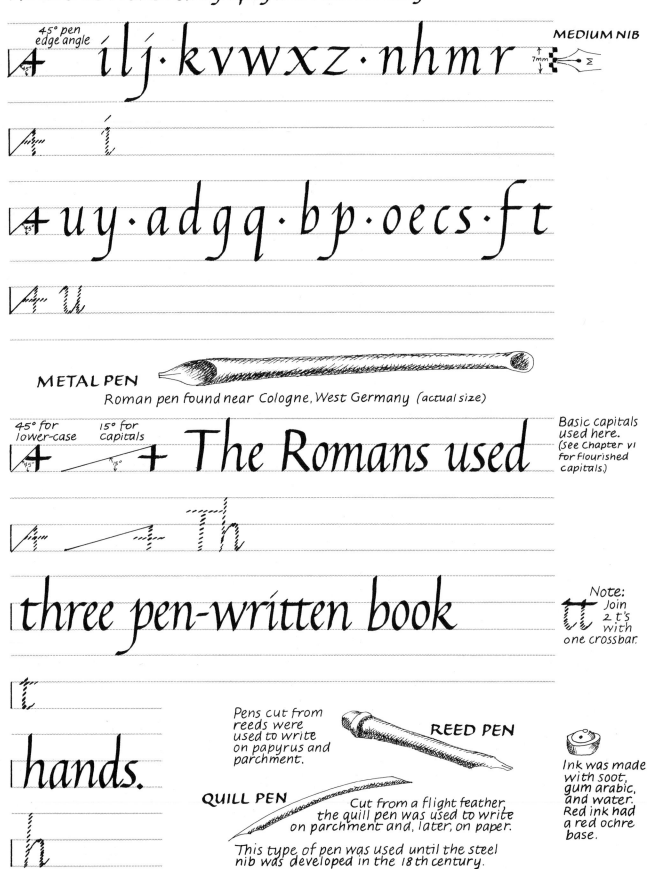

45° pen edge angle

ilj · kvwxz · nhmr

MEDIUM NIB

7mm

i

uy · adgq · bp · oecs · ft

u

METAL PEN

Roman pen found near Cologne, West Germany (actual size)

45° for lower-case

15° for capitals

The Romans used

Basic capitals used here. (See Chapter VI for flourished capitals.)

Th

three pen-written book

Note: Join 2 t's with one crossbar.

t

hands.

Pens cut from reeds were used to write on papyrus and parchment.

REED PEN

QUILL PEN

Cut from a flight feather, the quill pen was used to write on parchment and, later, on paper.

This type of pen was used until the steel nib was developed in the 18th century.

Ink was made with soot, gum arabic, and water. Red ink had a red ochre base.

h

FINE NIB

4 Square capitals and Rustic capitals were the

4.5

scripts used for books of poetry such as copies

5

LIBRADIESOMNIQ·PARE
ETMEDIVMIVCIAIQ·VM
EXERCETEVIRIIAVROSSI

of Virgil.

10

FELICESOPERVMQVINTAMIEVGEPAIIIDVSTIORCVS
EVMENIDESQVESATAETVMPARTVTERRANEEANDO·
COEVMQVELAPETVMQVECREATSAEVOMQVETYPHOEA
ETCONIVRATOSCAEIVMRESCINDEREFRATRES·
TERSVNICONATIINPONEREPELLOOSSAM

INCASTRAMADIAM ET
IOABRCUERSUSESTDE
POSTABENNER ETCON
GRAECARUNTTOTUM
POPULUM ETUISISUN
APUERISDAUIDDCCC
ETNOUEMPUERIS ETASA
EL ETPUERIDAUIDPERES

Uncial was the

u

script used for

5

writing copies

w

of the Bible.

10

Papyrus, made in Egypt, was used as a

P

writing surface by the

W

Egyptians, Greeks, and

E

Romans. Parchment was used by the Greeks

R

and Romans. Made from the skins of ani-

a

mals, it provided a durable, smooth surface.

m

Sheets of either papyrus or parchment were

s

PAPYRUS

rind removed

inner pith sliced into strips

Reeds often grow to a height of 10 feet.

After the stalks are cut, the thin strips are laid cross-wise—one layer horizontally and another layer vertically. A cloth is laid over the strips and the papyrus is rolled with a wooden tool. The two layers form one sheet of papyrus.

PARCHMENT

The earliest Greek parchment manuscript dates from the 2nd century B.C.

Parchment is made from sheepskin. Vellum is made from calfskin. Commonly all writing skins are called parchment.

SCROLL

A label (Latin-*TITULUS*) was attached to the end to identify.

Some scrolls were more than 30 meters long.

joined and rolled

j

into scrolls or folded in codices.

i

CODEX

Sheets were folded for easier storing and transporting

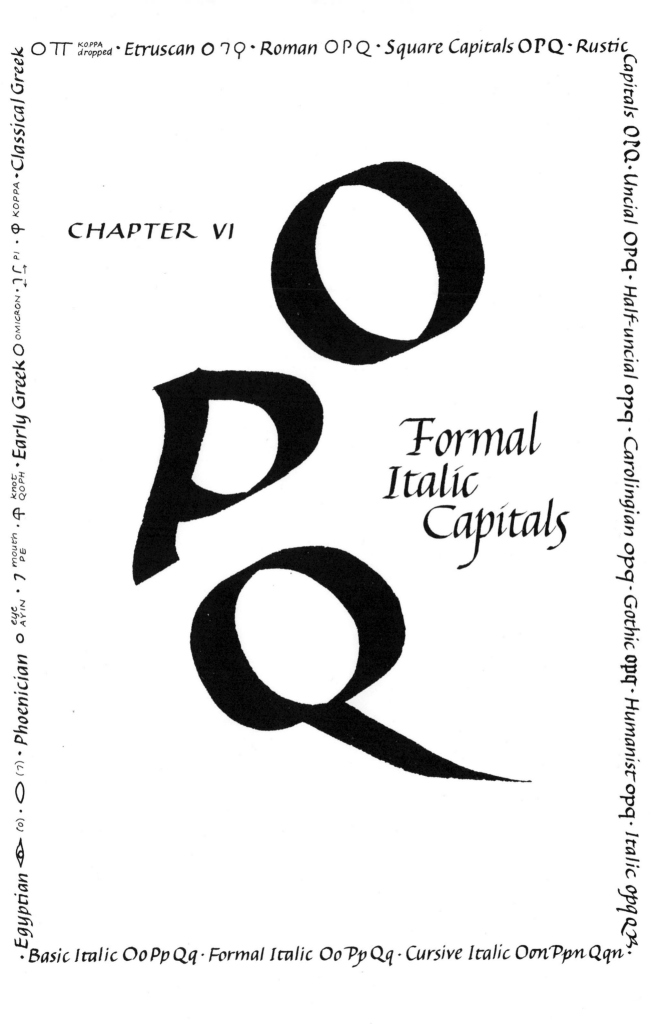

O TT KOPPA dropped · Etruscan O ꓶꓙ · Roman O P Q · Square Capitals OPQ · Rustic

Capitals OPQ · Uncial OPQ · Half-uncial opq · Carolingian opq · Gothic opq · Humanist opq · Italic opq Qᵧ

Egyptian ⟨o⟩ · ⟨ʔ⟩ · Phoenician O eye AYIN · 7 mouth PE · P knot QOPH · Early Greek O OMICRON · 7 ᴄ PI · φ KOPPA · Classical Greek

CHAPTER VI

Formal
Italic
Capitals

· Basic Italic Oo Pp Qq · Formal Italic Oo Pp Qq · Cursive Italic Oon Ppn Qqn ·

FORMAL CAPITALS
These letterforms are based on the Roman capitals (see Trajan Inscription, p. 42, and basic capitals, pp. 36 & 37). These formal capitals are enhanced with flourishes.

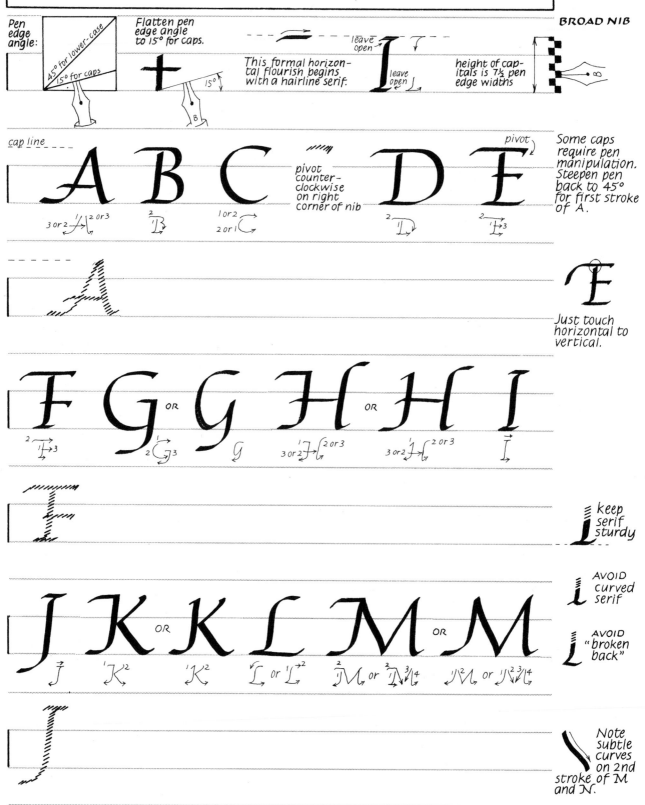

Pen edge angle: 45° for lower-case 15° for caps.

Flatten pen edge angle to 15° for caps.

This formal horizontal flourish begins with a hairline serif.

leave open

height of capitals is 7½ pen edge widths

BROAD NIB

cap line

Some caps require pen manipulation. Steepen pen back to 45° for first stroke of A.

3 or 2   2 or 3   1 or 2   2 or 1   pivot counter-clockwise on right corner of nib   pivot

Just touch horizontal to vertical.

keep serif sturdy

AVOID curved serif

AVOID "broken back"

Note subtle curves on 2nd stroke of M and N.

Use formal capitals as initial letters in conjunction with lower-case. Do <u>not</u> write entire words with them.

BROAD NIB

cap height

Check pen edge angle:

15°

pivot as on C

Keep this angle sharp.

Keep serif angular — AVOID

no

flatten pen edge angle to 0° for stroke 2

FORMAL ITALIC CAPITALS WITH LOWER-CASE

Formal caps are written at a 5° letter slope to the right of the vertical and with a 15° pen edge angle.

Letter slope 5° to right of vertical.

Lower-case letters are written at the same 5° letter slope, but with a 45° pen edge angle to the writing line.

It is necessary to shift pen edge angle for each cap and lower-case letter.

BROAD NIB

Aa Bb Cc Dd 10mm

Trace the models before writing your own letters.

Ee Ff Gg Hh

Ii Jj Kk Ll

Only the first capital examples from pages 58 and 59 are used on these two pages because of space. Use the 10 mm sample ruled sheet, p. 126, to practice the other letterforms.

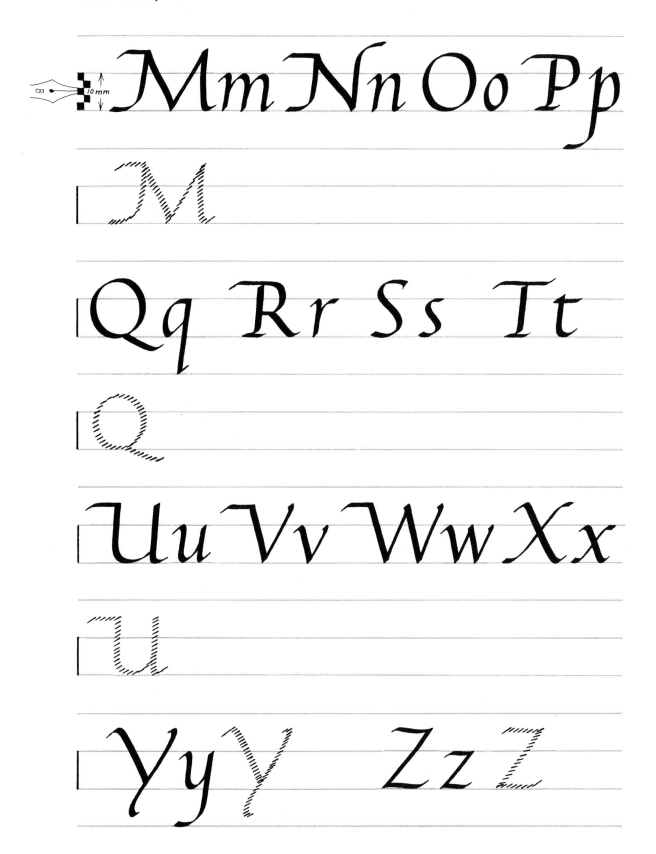

FORMAL ITALIC CAPITALS with lower-case
written with a medium (approximately 1½ mm) nib.

caps 15° lower-case 45°

MEDIUM NIB

Aa Bb Cc Dd Ee

Ff Gg Hh Ii Jj Kk

Note: Horizontals on E and F are only half as wide as the height of the letter.

Ll Mm Nn Oo Pp

N overlap strokes 2 and 3:

Qq Rr Ss Tt Uu Vv

Maintain strong horizontal on T.

(avoid T)

Ww Xx Yy & Zz

A + *The Roman half-uncial*

A + I

I *script develops the ascenders*

S

clamnationemfideierre
ceaboletur peraltran
rurrirabolendaert Cu
epircopimanuminnocente
guamnonadfulnloqiumcoe
·

ROMAN
HALF-UNCIAL
St. Hilary
Rome
before 509-10
(Biblioteca Vaticana,
Vatican City)
Reproduced by
permission.

I *and descenders.*

A

M *Monks in Ireland originated*

M

I *the Irish half-uncial.*

IRISH HALF-UNCIAL
Book of Kells
Ireland 800
(The Board of Trinity College, Dublin)
Reproduced by permission.

C

Occudiuic herdois Recinuuifes
uam eniin raccumeft homeni.

With a revival of learning

W

under Charlemagne' came a

Note:
Use flourish
on e on
occasion.

u

reform in writing resulting

Carolingian is
also called
Caroline
minuscule.

r

in the Carolingian script.

Square capitals,
Uncial, and
Rustic capitals
were used for
titles, headings,
and other uses
of capitals.

i

Et relicta ciuitate nazareth uenit et habitauit in caphar
naum maritimam. in finib; zabulon et nepthalim. ut
adimpleretur quod dictum e per esaiam prophetam;
terra zabulon et terra nepthalim · uia maris trans
iordanen galileae 'Gentium populus qui sedebat inte ·
nebris lucem uidit magnam · Et sedentibus in regio
ne umbraemoras lux ortae est;

CAROLINGIAN
Gospels: from
Prüm written
at Tours, France
9th century
LETTERING: MODES
OF WRITING IN
WESTERN EUROPE
FROM ANTIQUITY
TO THE END OF
THE 18TH CENTURY
by Hermann
Degering
(Taplinger/Pen-
talic, 1978)
Reproduced by
permission.

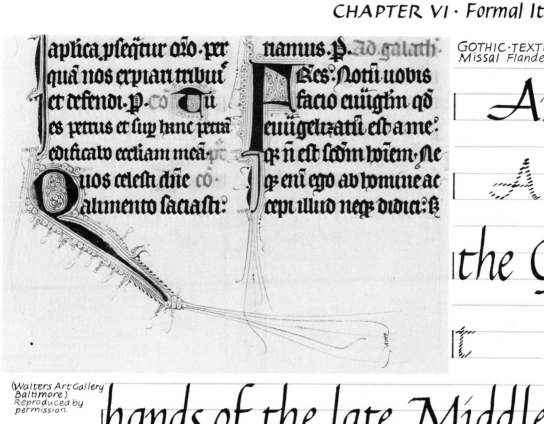

GOTHIC·TEXTUS QUADRATA
Missal Flanders 1300

Among

A

the Gothic

C

(Walters Art Gallery
Baltimore)
Reproduced by
permission.

hands of the late Middle Ages

Note:
This line is
very tightly
spaced.

In

Other Gothic
scripts were
Textus Prescis-
sus, Textus
Semiquadratus,
Fraktur, and
Gothic cur-
sive.
(Sometimes
Gothic is re-
ferred to as
Black Letter.)

were Textus Quadrata and

W

Rotunda.

R

GOTHIC·ROTUNDA
Missal, Italy 1500
LETTERING: MODES OF WRITING IN
WESTERN EUROPE FROM ANTIQUITY
TO THE END OF THE 18TH CENTURY
by Hermann Degering (Taplinger/
Pentalic, 1978). Reproduced by permission.

FINE NIB

45° lower-case pen edge angle

15° capital pen edge angle

The humanists (scholar/scribes of

the Italian Renaissance) studied and copied

classical Latin & Greek literature.   Impressed

by both the Carolingian hand of the manu-

scripts and the Gothic Rotunda hand influ-

ences, Francesco Petrarch, Coluccio Salutati,

Niccolò Niccoli, Poggio Bracciolini, and

others developed the Humanist script.

HUMANIST
Cicero
Poggio Bracciolini
Italy 1406
(Biblioteca Medici-
Laurenziana,
Florence, Italy)
Reproduced by permission.

posse non arbitrabar:ea dicta sunt a te: nec minus pla-

ne q̃ dicuntur a græcis: uerbis aptis. Sed tempus est si

uidetur: & recta quidem ad me. Quod cum ille dixis_

set: & satis disputatum uideretur: in oppidum ad pom_

A cursive version of the Humanist hand

A

HUMANISTIC
CURSIVE
Anonymous
scribe 1490
(The Houghton
Library, Harvard
University, Depart-
ment of Printing
& Graphic Arts)
Reproduced by
permission.

evolved in the 15th and 16th centuries as a

e

papa secundus Romanum imperium

in personam magnifici Caroli à Græcis

transtulit in Germanos. Alius ité Ro

manus Pontifex Zacharias scilicet

Regem Francorum non tam pro suis im

practical, rapidly written

p

script. Humanistic cursive

s

became known as cancellaresca, or chancery

b

cursive, and was written by, among others,

CANCELLARESCA
CORSIVA
(chancery cursive)
Writing book-
pen written
Italy 1545
(The Houghton
Library, Harvard
University, Depart-
ment of Printing
& Graphic Arts)
Reproduced by
permission.

C

Ludovico degli Arrighi & Bernardino Cataneo.

L

Non hauete à temer ch'informa nuoua Intagliare il mio cuor mai piu si possa

Se l'immagine uostra siritroua Scolpita in lui ch'esser non puo rimossa

Che il cuor non ho ducera & fatto proua Che li duc cento non ch'una percossa

Amor prima che scaglia neleuasse Quando l'immagin uostra lo ritrasse

Auorio ò gemma Et ogni pietra dura Che meglio da l'intaglio si diffende &

CAPITALS FOR CURSIVE ITALIC (CHAPTER VIII)

MONOLINE TOOL

Aa A A A A Bb B B Cc C Dd D D

Changes in the lower-case (shorter ascenders & descenders, serifs) are shown in detail in chapter VIII (see page 80).

Ee E E Ff F F Gg G Hh H H H

Ii I I I Jj J JJ Kk K K Ll L L

Mm M M Nn N N Oo O

Pp P P Qq Q Q Rr R R R R R

Ss S Tt T T T Uu U Vv V

Ww W Xx X X Yy Y Zz Z

B D E F P R T U Y H K

Modified flourishes as options

FINE NIB

4 Aa Bb Cc Dd Ee Ff Gg Hh Ii I

Capitals and lower-case are all written with a 45° pen edge angle for cursive italic.

Jj J Kk Ll L Mm Nn Oo Pp Qq

Note: Use same stroke sequence with edged pen as with monoline (above).

Rr R Ss Tt Uu Vv Ww Xx Yy Zz

CHAPTER VII

R
S
T

*Chancery
Italic*

Classical · SIGMA · Τ TAU
RHO
Early Greek ᕴ Ρ
mark TAU
tooth SHIN · W · X
head RESH
Phoenician ᕴ
Egyptian (٩) · (w) · (x)

CHANCERY ITALIC CAPITALS
In the 15th & 16th centuries, the chancery hand developed. The chancery was the office where official documents were kept & chancery was the official handwriting for these records.

Flatten pen edge angle to 15° for capitals.

Horizontal is now about ½ width of downstroke.

This chancery flourish is a rounded right angle – keep it sturdy.

Pull downward slightly before pushing up and over.

leave open

leave open

cap height

BROAD NIB

steepen pen for stroke 1

cap line

pivot counter-clockwise on right corner of nib

pivot

You may omit horizontal at left of downstroke on E and F.

cap line

Just touch B horizontal to vertical.

Avoid weak rounded serif - keep it sturdy.

YES

Keep all horizontal serifs flat.

Note extension to right of downstroke only 1 pen width.

NO   AVOID curved serif

NO   AVOID "broken back"

Note subtle curves on 2nd stroke of M and N.

It is characteristic of the italic capitals that when the flourishes are removed, the basic Roman shapes remain.

Use chancery italic capitals with lower-case only. Do *not* write entire words with them.

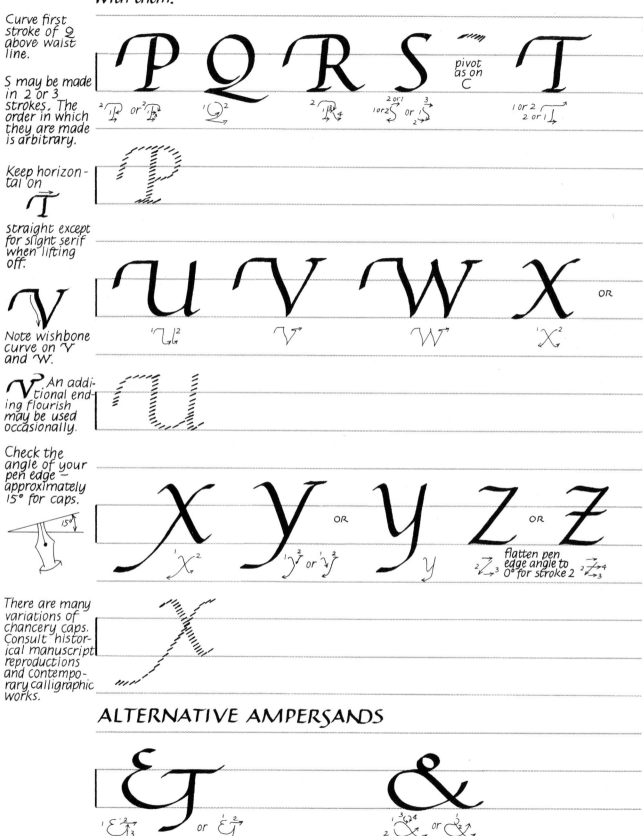

Curve first stroke of Q above waist line.

S may be made in 2 or 3 strokes. The order in which they are made is arbitrary.

Keep horizontal on T straight except for slight serif when lifting off.

Note wishbone curve on V and W.

An additional ending flourish may be used occasionally.

Check the angle of your pen edge — approximately 15° for caps.

There are many variations of chancery caps. Consult historical manuscript reproductions and contemporary calligraphic works.

pivot as on C

flatten pen edge angle to 0° for stroke 2

ALTERNATIVE AMPERSANDS

CHANCERY ITALIC LOWER-CASE
Formal italic lower-case letters with additional flourishes

The chancery serif is a flowing curve formed by rounding off a right angle.

formal italic   chancery italic

You may wish to pull your pen edge slightly right, then push left to cause pen to flow smoothly.

Note:
1 The flourished ascender extends only the width of h or b.
2 Curve occurs in upper half of space between waist line and ascender line.

BROAD NIB

10 mm

The chancery serif is formed on:

b, d, h, k, & l.

The f maintains its original curve.

Note:
At first it may be difficult to judge the width of the serifs on d and l. It may help to visualize an h.

Avoid:

h   h

weak serifs— not as wide as body of letter.

h   h

Avoid serif wider than body of letter.

Avoid square serif.

Two ff's and 2 ll's may be staggered in height.

The first l is at cap height.

y: Begin with a diagonal steeper than v, then abruptly curve at base line.

(See p. 101 for other variations.)

CHANCERY ITALIC CAPITALS AND LOWER-CASE
written with a medium nib (approximately 1½ mm).

MEDIUM NIB

Shift pen edge angle from 15° for caps to 45° for lower-case.

Aa Bb Cc Dd Ee

Maintain a sharp angle on *H* and *K*.

The second downstroke of *H* may descend below the base line.

Ef Gg Hh Ii Jj Kk

Ll Mm Nn Oo Pp

Mastering these letterforms requires patience and practice. Use the sample ruled pages at the back of this book for further practice.

Qq Rr Ss Tt Uu Vv

Ww Xx Yy & Zz

e inclinati / vobis harum serie mandamus, ut eundem Guillermu ad legendum

...nibus et ordinationibus aplicis ceterisq contrarijs quibuscuneq · Datum Rome

Humanistic cursive developed

HUMANISTIC
CURSIVE
*Brief of Pope
Sixtus IV
Italy 1480*

H

into cancellaresca,

i

or chancery cursive,

o

CANCELLARESCA
*Brief of
Pope Leo X
Italy 1515*

used for writing

u

papal briefs.

CANCELLARESCA
*Brief of Pope Clement VII
Italy 1530
Papal briefs reproduced by permission.
(Archives Nationales Bibliothèque, Paris)*

LVI.

non erat aßumpsit: non commixti
onem paßus neqз diuisionem . ad ﬔ
magnificat et ad Nunc dimittis an
tiph **M**agnum hereditatis mysteri
um : templum dei factus est uterus
nesciens uirum. non est pollutus ex
ea carnem aßumens. omnes gentes
uenient dicentes **G**loria tibi Dñe ﬔ
N ota, a uesperis sabbati sancti usqs
ad ascensionem dici officium beatæ
Mariæ sicut ante aduentum: nisi
qd' ad benedictus : ad magnificat : &
nunc dimittis dicitur antiphona
R egina celi letare : alleluia : quia
quem meruisti portare alleluia : re'
surrexit sicut dixit alleluia . Ora
pro nobis Deum
alleluia
A D M I S S A M .

CANCELLARESCA FORMATA
Hours of the B.V.M., Italy 1530-40
Made for the wife of the Duke of Urbino
(Bodleian Library, Oxford, MS. Douce 29, folio 55 recto)
Reproduced by permission.

Cancellaresca was

c

also a book hand

a

written in for-

w

mal, unjoined &

m

Note:
hyphen
variation

upright ver-

u

UPRIGHT
ITALIC SCRIPT
Psalter
Italy 1515
Made for the
Duke of Nemours
(Bodleian Library,
Oxford,
MS. Montagu e.9
folio 127 verso)
Reproduced by
permission.

sions.

antate domino canticum
nouum: cantate domino
omnis terra .
antate dño et benedicite nomini eius:
annunciate' de die in diem salutare eius .
nnunciate inter gentes gliam eius: in
omnibus pphs mirabilia eius .
uoniam magnus dominus et lauda-
bilis nimis terribilis super omnes deos.

Ludovico degli Arrighi

FINE NIB

L

wrote the first manual of the

W

chancery hand, LA OPERINA,

C

printed from woodcut letters

P

in Rome in the year 1522.

i

Others, such as Giovanbattista

O

Palatino

Vltra le retro=
scritte cinque littere a c d g g
ti fo intendere
che anchora quasi tutte le altre lre
se hanno á formare in questo :: qua=
dretto oblungo et non quadro per
fetto □
perche alocchio mio la littera
corsiua ouero Cancellarescha
vuole hauere
del
lungo & non del rotondo : che rotonda
ti veneria fatta quá=
do dal quadro
perfetto
& non oblungo la formasti

Egli è il uero, che io hò amato, et amo Guiscardo, et quáto io uiue
ro, che sará poco, lamero, et se appresso la morte sama, non mi ri
marró damarlo, à questo non mindusse tanto la mia feminile fragilitá,
quanto la tua poca sollecitudine del maritarmi, & la uertú dilui es
ser ti doueua. Tancredi manifesto, essendo tu di carne, hauete genera
ta figliuola di carne, & non di pietra ò di ferro, & ricordarti doueui

and Giovanantonio Tagliente, also wrote

a

writing books printed from

w

Le lettere cancellaresche sopranominate se fanno tonde
longe large tratizzate e non tratizzate ET per che io
to scritto questa variacione de lettera la qual im-
parcraj secundo li nostri precetti et opere

relief wood blocks.

r

A a/a b c d c e f g h i k l m n o p q r s s t u x y z &

CANCELLARESCA
CORSIVA
Writing book
OPERA CHE
INSEGNA A
SCRIVERA
Tagliente
Italy 1524
(Newberry Library,
Chicago)
Reproduced by
permission.

The first writing book published in England,

T

A BOOKE CONTAINING DIVERS SORTES OF HANDS,

A

called the chancery hand the "italique hande."

c

ITALIC
Preface of
Plutarch
Sir John Cheke
Cambridge
1544-46
(The Master and
Fellows of Univer-
sity College, Oxford,
MS. Univ. Coll. 171
folio 32)
Reproduced by
permission.

Italic was the script of Elizabethan courtiers

q

in factis dissimulatio sit, sed omnibus partibus recte
integreq constitutis non manci apud deum truncu
religionis particula habeamur, sed absoluti et per-
fecti, corde integro reperiamur. Dominus Jesus
Maiestatem tuam florentissimam seruet. Hart-
fordie, 30 Decembris

and of scholars

a

such as Sir John

s

Cheke. c

Parchment and vellum were used for books until the 14th & 15th centuries, when they began to be replaced by paper.

P

Paper was invented by the Chinese in the 1st century A.D., but it wasn't until the 12th century that paper (made from cotton or linen rags) was used in Europe. With the advent of printing with movable type in the 15th century paper was in great demand.

P

The Chinese made paper from plant fibers such as mulberry and gampi.

WESTERN METHOD
Small pieces of cotton or linen rags are beaten in water to form a pulp. More water is added to the pulp in a vat.

DECKLE
MOLD

Deckle frame fits over the mold. The mold and deckle are immersed in the vat to gather a thin layer of pulp on the mold.

VAT OF PULP

The deckle is then removed and the mold with the layer of pulp is turned over and rolled onto a piece of felt.

FELT
PULP

After being pressed, dried, and sized a piece of paper is ready to be written on.

CHAPTER VIII

Cursive Italic
Handwriting

u · w *7th century: Anglo-Saxon. · Humanist u · Italic u · The round form of v (u) became the regular form; the sharp form v was used only occasionally. 11th century to England · Modern distinctions made in 16th–17th centuries when capital u & lower-case u were added.*

CURSIVE ITALIC LOWER-CASE

The word cursive comes from the Latin CURRERE (to run).
Join lower-case letters using 8 join families. The dotted
lines indicate the various ways letters are joined together.

JOIN 1
an

JOIN 2
au

JOIN 3
ao

JOIN 4
en

JOIN 5
on

JOIN 6
rn

JOIN 7
sn

JOIN 8
aa

To facilitate joining and increase speed, ascenders and
descenders are shortened (similar to basic italic).

MONOLINE TOOL

short ascenders

bb dd ff hh kk ll

1 stroke

short descenders

ff gg jj pp qq yy

1 stroke

no entrance serif for i, u & y   sharp entrance serif for v & w

serif changes to facilitate joining

ii uu yy   vv ww

serif stops at waist line ↓   2nd stroke straight line   Curve ending of r slightly (so it will not look like v when written rapidly).

other changes

pp xx rr

SUGGESTED PAPER POSITIONS FOR CURSIVE ITALIC HANDWRITING

Right-handed

If you are right-handed, slant your book slightly to the left.

Left-handed

If you are left-handed and write with your wrist below the line of writing, slant your book slightly to the right.

If you are left-handed and write with a "hook" with your wrist above the line of writing, slant your book slightly to the left.

JOIN 1 · DIAGONAL ROLLOVER
Join with a diagonal line, then roll over
into n, m, r, and x.

an · an am ar ax

Join out of letters ending with base-line serifs
a, c, d, h, i, k, l, m, n, u, and z.

Join out of a
or c, d, h, i, k,
l, m, n, u & z.

an an am ar ax

an

an · an cn dn hn in kn ln mn nn un zn

an

Note height of
capitals (see
cursive capitals
page 68).

Ann Dan Ian or *Jan Jan* or *Jan Nan Van*

A

am · am cm dm hm im km lm mm nm

am

um zm · Cam Jim Kim Pam Sam Tim

um

ar · ar cr dr hr ir kr lr mr nr ur zr

ar

NOTE:
straight diagonal line

an

Note that
A & B are
two different shapes.

slightly rounded angle

ax or *ax*
OPTION
serifs on
2nd stroke

ax ix ux · Max

ax

AVOID:
wavy join

an

A & B too similar
in shape (n doesn't have
two arches)

scoop

ax · Max · ax

JOIN 2 · DIAGONAL SWINGUP
Join with a diagonal line, then swing up
into u, y, i, t, j, p, v, w, l, h, k, and b.

au · au ay ai at aj ap
av aw al ah ab ak

Join out of letters ending with base-line serifs
a, c, d, h, i, k, l, m, n, u, and z.

au au ay ai at aj ap

au

av aw al ah ab ak

av

au cu du hu iu ku lu mu nu uu zu   au

au

ay cy dy hy iy ky ly my ny uy · Ray   ay

ay

ai ci di hi ii ki li mi ni ui zi · Mimi   ai

ai

Amy Kay Jimmy
A
Tammy T

NOTE:
blend at center
au
slightly rounded angle

AVOID:
blend too low
au
scoop

at | at ct dt ht it kt lt mt nt ut · Kit Pat

at

Note double t is 2 strokes. | tt tt tt Matt · tt

aj ap | aj ij uj · ap cp dp hp ip kp lp mp np up · Kip

aj

av
aw | av iv lv mv uv · aw iw mw uw · Liv

av

al | al cl dl hl il kl ll ml nl ul zl · Bill Hal

al

Emily Gail Jill Lily Milt Paul Sally

E

ah
ab
ak | ah ch ih uh · ab ib mb ub · ak ck ik kk

ah

lk nk uk · Lib Hank Kiku Wah

ik

NOTE:

blend slightly above center for v & w

av

slightly rounded angle

single line above waist line — blend at center for ascenders (or slightly above)

at

slightly rounded angle

AVOID:

blend too low

aw

scoop

double line above waist line — loop

al al

scoop

AVOID SCOOP & LOOP

Phillip Elijah

P

Quynh Willy

Q

Nahum Saul

N

Emil Milly

E

JOIN 3 · DIAGONAL STARTBACK
Join with a diagonal line, then start back down
into o, e, and s.

ao · ao ae as

Join out of letters ending with base-line serifs
a, c, d, h, i, k, l, m, n, u, and z.

ao ao ae ae as *leave off top of s*

ao

ao co do ho io ko lo mo no uo zo · Kao   ao
ao   ao

ae ce de he ie ke le me ne ue ze · Sue   ae
ae   ae

Anne Jane June Lane Luke Mike
A

as cs ds hs is ks ls ms ns us zs · Luis   as
as   as

Willis Linus Lue
W

Aline Dale Julie
A

Julius Lyle Pao
J

Cammie Jimmie
C

NOTE:

straight diagonal line—follow back down
⅓ of diagonal join

ao ae as

slightly rounded angle   *leave open*   *leave off horizontal top of s when joined from base line*

AVOID:

wavy join line   *follows back down too far*

ao ae as as
scoop *scoop* *scoop* *closes up*

84

JOIN 4 · DIAGONAL OUT OF E
Join with a diagonal line following back out
of 2nd stroke of e into all letters except f (lift before f).

en · en eu eo ea ez

en en eu eo ea ez   · ef

en

en · en em er ex · Alex Clem Elmer Glenn

en

eu · eu ey ei et ej ep ev ew el eh eb ek · Bev

eu

Helen Huey Janet Lev Lew Neil Zeke

H

eo · eo ee es · Leo Lee Les Miles Queenie

eo

ea ez · ea ec ed eg eq es · ez · Bea Peg Ted · Inez

ea

James with top of s OR James without top of s

J

Dean Jean Ned

D

Renée Theo Tieu

R

NOTE: diagonal line with slight curve
en eu
follow back out from center

AVOID: join not following 2nd stroke back out from center
en   eu
scoop   2nd stroke too low

JOIN 5 · HORIZONTAL
Join with a horizontal line out of o, t, f, v, w, and x
into all letters except f (*lift before f*).

on · on tn fn vn wn xn

---

on on ou oo oa ot ol oz · of

on

on om or ox · Dion Jon Ron Thor Tom   on

ou oy oi oj op ov ow · oo oe · Joe Joy Lois   ou
ou   oo

oa oc od og oq os · Joab Joan Rodney   oa
oa

ot ot · ol oh ob ok · oz · Bob Dot John   ot ol
ol   oz

Colleen Elliott Floyd   **NOTE:**
C

Helon Lionel Lloyd   *straight horizontal line*
H   ou ol

Naomi Rollo Toni
N   **AVOID:**

Solomon S   *scoop*   *diagonal rather than horizontal*
          ou   ol

tn tn tu to ta tl tz · tf · tt

tn

tn tn tm tr tx · tu ty ti tj tp tv tw · to te · Peter

tn

tu to tn

ta tl ta tc td tg tq ts · tl th tb tk · tz · tf · tt · Mitzi

ta

NOTE:

straight horizontal crossbar

tn tl

open
curve at baseline
slightly narrower
with cursive italic t

AVOID:

scoop   diagonal

tn tl

curve too wide

Betty Kathy Ruth
B
Matthew Stanley
M

fn fn fu fo fa ft or ft fl fz · ff

fn

fn fn fm fr fx · fu fy fi fj fp fv fw · fo fe · Alfie

fn

fu fo
fa fl fa fc fd fg fq fs · ft or ft · fl fh fb fk · fz · ff

fa

Afton Clifton
A
Rafael Rufus
R

NOTE:

fn fl

straight horizontal crossbar

AVOID:

fn fl

scoop   diagonal

vn vn vu vo va vt vl vz

vn

JOIN 5
(continued)

*Join out of
v into all
letters
except f
(lift before f).*

va ve vi vo vu · Aviva Dave Eva Ivan

va

Ivar Kevin Levi Olive Steven Yvonne

I

vn

wn wu wo wa wt wl wz

wn

*Join out of
w into all
letters
except f
(lift before f).*

wa we wi wo wu · Gwen Lewis Newton

wa

wn

xn xn xu xo xa xt xl xz

xn

*Join out of
x into all
letters
except f
(lift before f).*

xa xe xi xo xu · Axel Dexter Roxie

xa

xn

NOTE:

straight horizontal line

vn

*diagonal blends into
horizontal*

wn xn

AVOID: *no horizontal*

vn

scoop

wn

no horizontal

xn xn

scoop *scoop*

JOIN 6 · DIAGONAL OUT OF R
Join with a short diagonal line out of r
into all letters except f.

rn · rn rn ru ro ra rz

rn · rn or rn ru ro ra rz · rf

rn

rn rm rr rx or rn rm rr rx · Arne Carmen
rn

ru ry ri rt rj rp rv rw rt rh rb rk · Arthur
ru

Carlos Cherie Erin Harry Henry Marie
C

ro re rs · ra rc rd rg rq rs · rz · Corazon
ro

Carol Larry Laura Mara Sara Vera
C

Catherine Karen
C

Karl Leonora Lars
K

Mary Marcus
M

Shirley S

NOTE:

r curves down slightly, then
joins with a
short diagonal
line

ru

AVOID:

no curve down
(looks
like
vu)

ru

scoop

ru

pointed

ru

JOIN 7 · HORIZONTAL TO DIAGONAL
*Join with a horizontal line, following back out
of s, b, and p, blending into a diagonal line.*

sn · sn bn pn

Join into all letters except f (lift before f).

sn · sn bn pn · sf

sn sm sr sx · su sy si st sj sp sv sw sl sh sb sk   *sn*

su

so se ss · Jess Jessie José Justin Louise   *so*

bn br · bu by bi bt bl bb · bo be bs · Alberta   *bn*

bu

Bobby Deborah Gabriel Robert Wilbur   *bo*

pn pr · pu py pi pt pp pl pb · po pe ps · Hope   *pn*

pu

Christopher Joseph Ralph Stephen   *po*

NOTE:

sn bn

↑follow back out↑

AVOID:

sn bn   sn bn

(no horizontal)   double scoop

JOIN 8 · DIAGONAL TO HORIZONTAL
Join with a diagonal line blending into a horizontal
line. Start back on horizontal to begin a,c,d,g & q.

a·a · aa ac ad ag aq

Join out of letters ending with base-line serifs:
a, c, d, h, i, k, l, m, n, u, and z; also out of b, p, and s.

---

aa · aa ac ad ag aq

aa

aa   aa ca da ha ia ka la ma na ua za · Juana
aa

ac   ac cc ic uc · ad dd id ld nd ud · Alice Todd
ad   ac

ag   ag ig ug · aq iq uq · ba pa sa · Quang Aataq
aq   ag

Barbara Charles David Jonathan Lisa
B

Michael Michelle Monica Nancy Tia
M

NOTE: aa *maintain horizontal*

Nick Philippa Sasha Susan
N

AVOID: aa *wavy join, horizontal missing, scoop*

Ursula Vincent Wendy
U

aa

Yolanda Y

NO JOIN · *Lift before f.*
Lift before z from base line.
Lift after g, j, q, and y.

af · az · ga ja qu ya

Lift to avoid loops, thereby maintaining legibility.

af · az · ga ja qu ya

af

NOTE: *Space letters closely when lifts occur. A join is a natural spacer, so when no join occurs consistent spacing must be maintained.*

af ef if of uf · Alf Cliff Olaf Ulf Winifred
af

af

az iz uz zz · Elizabeth Liza Lizzie Shizuko
az

az

Lift after a, c, d, h, i, k, l, m, n, u, and z before z.

ga ge gg gi go gu · Gregory Helge Inga
ga

ga

ja je ji jo ju · qu · ya ye yi yo yu · Jacqueline
ja

ja

Anya Bryant Joyce Quyen Sonja Sylvia
A

qu

ya

A quick brown fox jumps over the lazy dog. **PANGRAM**
A

92

FINE NIB

REVIEW · CURSIVE ITALIC JOINS

JOIN 1 · Diagonal rollover into n,m,r & x out of a,c,d,h,i,k,l,m,n,u & z.

an am ar ax · an

JOIN 2 · Diagonal swingup into u,y,i,t,j,p,v,w,l,h,b & k out of a,c,d,h,i,k,l,m,n,u & z.

au ay ai at aj ap av aw al ah ab ak

au

JOIN 3 · Diagonal startback into o,e & s out of a,c,d,h,i,k,l,m,n,u & z.

ao ae as · ao

JOIN 4 · Diagonal out of e into all letters except f.

en eu eo ea ez · en

JOIN 5 · Horizontal out of o,t,f,v,w & x into all letters except f.

on tn fn vn wn xn · (on ou oo oa ot ol oz)

on

JOIN 6 · Diagonal out of r into all letters except f.

rn ru ro ra rz · rn

JOIN 7 · Horizontal to diagonal out of s,b & p into all letters except f.

sn bn pn su bu pu so bo po

sn

JOIN 8 · Diagonal to horizontal into a,c,d,g & q out of a,c,d,h,i,k,l,m,n,u & z.

aa ac ad ag aq · aa

NO JOIN · Lift before f and before z from base line. Lift after g,j,q & y.

af az · ga ja qu ya · af

FOR JOIN VARIATIONS SEE CHAPTER IX, PAGES 106

**PRACTICE
EXERCISE**

ana bnb cnc dnd ene fnf gng hnh ini

a

jnj knk lnl mnm nnn ono pnp qnq rnr

j

For further
practice vary
the constant
letter (see n
in exercise).

sns tnt unu vnv wnw xnx yny & znz

y

The word cursive comes from the Latin CURRERE (to run). Cursive writing is characterized by slightly sloped elliptical letterforms. Letters are written with few strokes and are often joined. In the Roman Empire, Roman cursive was used for business and correspondence.

The quickly written letters were scratched on walls, on clay, wax, or wooden tablets or written on papyrus.

ROMAN CURSIVE
*Wall inscription (graffiti)
Pompeii
1st century* A.D.
A HANDBOOK OF GREEK AND LATIN PALAEOGRAPHY *by* E.L.Thompson
(Ares Publishers Inc. Chicago, 1966)
Reproduced by permission.

ROMAN CURSIVE
*Deed of sale
Ink on papyrus strip 1' x 8'6"
Rimini, Italy 572*
(British Library, London)
Reproduced by permission.

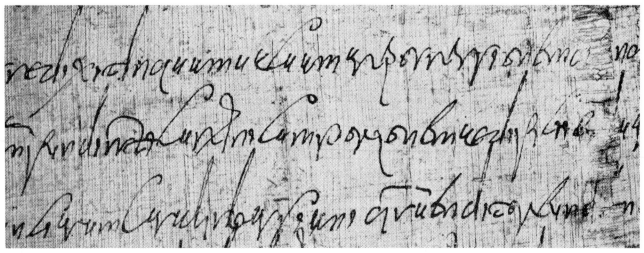

Roman cursive eventually degenerated into an illegible scrawl and was suppressed

**Frederick II
Roman emperor,
king of Sicily and
Jerusalem**

by order of Frederick II in the year 1220. In

**SECRETARY
Document on
vellum
England 1616
(James F. Hayes)
Reproduced by
permission.**

northern Europe Gothic cursive (Secretary)

evolved & was in use until the 19th century.

**SECRETARY
Portion of letter
from Henry VIII
(age 27) to
Cardinal Wolsey
England 1518
(British Library,
London)**

("Wrytten
with the hand
off your loving
master HENRY R")

**"The All But Lost
Art of Handwriting"
by Wolf Von Eckardt
HORIZON, Vol. II, No.1
(American Heritage
Publishing Company,
New York)
Reproduced by
permission.**

After the invention of movable type most

books were no longer written by hand. Yet

commercial, legal, and private writing

needs remained. In Italy, Humanistic cur-

sive (italic)

served as

the per-

sonal hand of many; it also fit the secretar-

ial needs of the Chancery (see p.67 & p.74). In England,

the "italique hande" was used by scholars (see p.97),

HUMANISTIC
CURSIVE (ITALIC)
Letter from
Michelangelo
Italy 1549
(The Pierpont
Morgan Library,
New York)
Reproduced by
permission.

secretaries

& royalty.

Writing masters were becoming competi-

tive, often trying to outdo one another with

ITALIC
Letter from
Princess
Elizabeth
(age 15) to
Protector
Somerset
England 1548-9
(Bodleian Library,
Oxford, MS Ashmole
1729, folio 152)
Reproduced by
permission.

a "command of hand." The resulting script, a

round hand (copperplate), required great r

calligraphic skill. Writing manuals were c

abbcddefoghhijkkllllmnnoppqrsfstuvnxyz.
ABCDEFGHIJKLMMM
NNOP2RSTUVWXXYYZ.

BURIN

Sharp metal tool for cutting (engraving) letters on copper plate. It can make the thinnest or thickest of lines.

printed from engraved copper plates, the p

letters written with a burin, not a pen. v

POINTED STEEL NIB

Dip nib for writing with ink on paper. With pressure sharp point widens for thick lines.

To imitate the engraver's art, a point- T

ed steel nib was used for pen-written e

round r
hand. n
Thins & t

thicks were achieved by continually varying t

pressure on the nib. p

The first writing book published in

America was by John Jenkins in 1791

and was based on round hand, the script

for official documents. In

1848 Platt Rogers Spencer

wrote BUSINESS PENMANSHIP.

At the turn of the century Charles Zaner

and Austin Palmer published their ver-

sions of commercial cursive scripts.

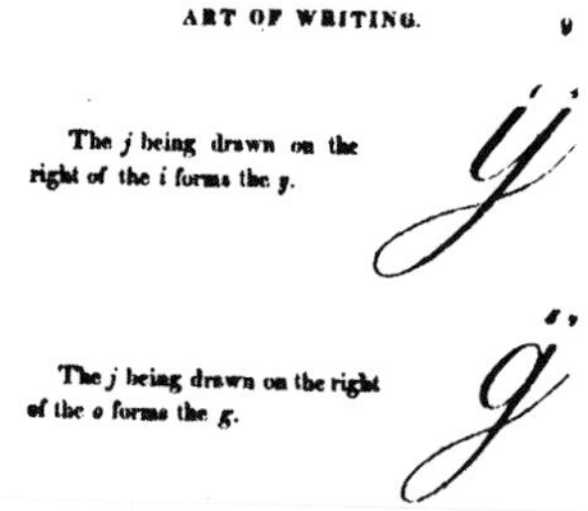

The present revival of calligraphy and italic handwriting is based on the letter designs of the Renaissance. The italic forms provide us with a graceful, fluent, and practical script for our day.

ART OF WRITING.

The *j* being drawn on the right of the *i* forms the *y*.

The *j* being drawn on the right of the *o* forms the *g*.

ROUND HAND
ART OF WRITING
by John Jenkins
America 1791

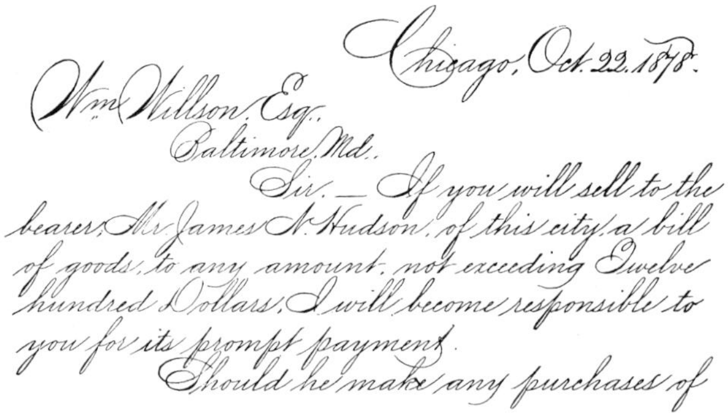

Chicago, Oct. 22, 1878.

Wm Wilson Esq.
Baltimore Md.
Sir.— If you will sell to the bearer, Mr James N Hudson, of this city, a bill of goods, to any amount, not exceeding Twelve hundred Dollars, I will become responsible to you for its prompt payment.
Should he make any purchases of

COMMERCIAL CURSIVE
A specimen of Spencerian Business Writing from an 1879 version of WHO'S WHO IN AMERICA
Examples of Jenkins' round hand & Spencerian business writing from HANDWRITING MODELS FOR SCHOOLS by Charles Lehman (Alcuin Press, Portland, Oregon, 1976). Reproduced by permission.

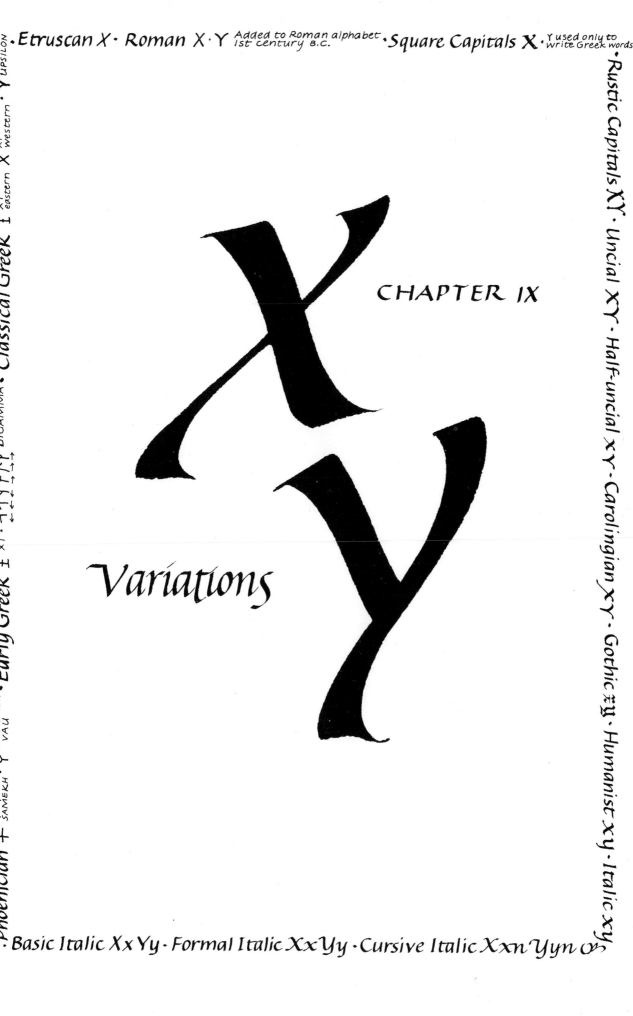

CHAPTER IX

Variations

Classical Greek Ⲭ ΧΙ eastern Χ ΧΙ western · Υ UPSILON

Early Greek Ⲭ ΧΙ · ꓩꓶꓘ Fᖴꓗꓩ DIGAMMA ·

Phoenician ⴲ prop SAMEKH · Υ hook·nail VAU ·

Rustic Capitals XY· Uncial XY · Half-uncial xy · Carolingian xy · Gothic ẍy · Humanist xy · Italic xy

·Basic Italic Xx Yy · Formal Italic Xx Yy · Cursive Italic Xxn Yyn Oy·

VARIATIONS
weight, height, pen edge angle, modified serifs
In this book italic is generally written at a 5° letter slope with a pen edge
angle to the writing line of 45° for lower-case letters and 15° for caps.
Here are some alternatives.

MEDIUM NIB

narrow and compressed letters

standard 5° letter slope written at 5 pen edge widths

wide and expanded italic

standard 5° letter slope written at 5 pen edge widths

vertical · narrow · wide

an upright italic written at 5 pen edge widths

a 15° slope · narrow · wide

5 pen edge widths, letter slope about 15° to the right

italic at 4 pen edge widths

When preparing a layout that will be reduced photographically – a greeting card, an announcement, address labels – try 4 pen edge widths. The letters will appear stronger.

italic written at 3 pen edge widths

lightweight italic

7 pen edge widths

italic written at 30°

vertical modified italic

5 pen edge widths (See p. 105.)

modified italic written at 2½ pen edge widths

modified italic at 6 widths

FLOURISHES, DOUBLE CONSONANTS, ALTERNATIVE SERIFS, GOTHIC FLOURISH

Use these vari-ations with formal or chan-cery italic. (Do _not_ overuse.)

MEDIUM NIB

· e e e e ⟶ Dunmore

Note:
When stagger-ing ff, the 1st f begins at cap height, halfway between the base and waist lines.

· ff ff ff fl fl Jefferson

gg Extend 2nd stroke over into counter of 1st g.

· gg gg g gg Eggleston

g Use as a single or double consonant.

· ck Suffolk · ll Hillsboro

Use flourished n at the end of a line or sentence. May also use with a, d, h, m or u. Flatten pen edge for flourish. Use flourished p as a single or double con-sonant.

one stroke ↰

· n Adrian · pp Heppner

Lowered s is also used as single consonant.

· ss Moss · ℰt ſt Thurston

ℰt (ct) and ſt (st): 16th-century ligatures (See p. 33).

ALTERNATIVE SERIFS:

BRACKET SERIF
("bird beak serif")

l or l or l bd hkl Midland

SIMPLE SERIF
(added to ascenders)

Use with formal lower-case only—just a hint of a serif. Don't exaggerate!

l bd hkl Bloomfield

GOTHIC FLOURISH

For certificates, announcements & the like. Use with lower-case, _not_ as all caps.

Vertical line may touch base line or extend beyond.

B C D E K R T

Also may be added to F, G, H, I, J, L, M, N, O, P, Q, and U.

VERTICAL CAPITALS
Use vertical capitals for titles, headings, posters, announcements, or quotations. Use ruled sheets provided to practice these letters.

MONOLINE · 1½ spaces high using the 10 mm ruled sheet.

O Q C G G D

A H K N T U

V X Y Z · E F L J

B P R R S · I · M W

Vertical caps made with the monoline tool and edged pen maintain the same letter widths that were introduced in Chapter III.

They are based on the Roman incised letterforms.

Two forms of G and R are shown.

MONOLINE VERTICAL CAPS

EDGED PEN · 7½ pen edge widths high using the 10 mm ruled sheet.
BROAD NIB

15°

O Q C G G D

A H K N T U

V X Y Z · E F L J

B P R R S · I · M W

Maintain a 15° pen edge angle for these caps as well as all others introduced in this book.

Steepen your pen for:
1. 1st stroke of A.
2. All strokes of N.
3. 1st stroke of M.

Flatten pen edge angle for upper diagonal of K and diagonal of Z.

EDGED PEN VERTICAL CAPS

SLAB SERIF CAPITALS
Use these caps when serifs are desired. All other flourished caps (pp. 57-68 and 69-78, Chapters VI and VII) are to be used ONLY in conjunction with lower-case. Maintain BASIC CAP widths, p. 36.

Write at 7½ or 8 pen edge widths using 10 mm ruled sheet.

BROAD NIB

A slab is a thin horizontal line added to vertical or diagonal strokes.

Flatten your pen to about 10° for slabs.

Generally extend slab 1 pen edge width on either side of stroke.

O Q C G D ·

A H K N T U

V X Y Z · E F L J

B P R R S · I · M W

These capitals also may be written vertically.

MEDIUM NIB

5 pen edge widths

EDGED PEN SLAB SERIFS

7½ pen edge widths

USE SLAB SERIFS AS ALL CAPS

Use basic or slab serif caps to write entire words.

Use slab serif caps with italic lower-case formal italic.

Write them with lower-case letters.

Use large and small caps together.

COMBINE LARGE & SMALL

FREE CAPS
   Free caps have a non-rigid rhythmic line. The pen edge angle changes when pivoting or twisting.
   (These caps were used as the large letters in the chapter headings.)

Basic strokes: 5 pen edge widths

Downstroke curves slightly right, then left of the basic cap letterform.

Twist pen for the ending serifs of some letters.

5 mm nib

Hunt's Speedball C-O nib used to write this page.

Use any 5 mm nib.

Maintain 15°–30° pen edge angle except when pivoting or twisting.

Use tracing paper to copy letters.

A B C D E

A – sans serif ending, or use
B – pivot serif

Pivot on the base-line for B, D, and E.

F G H I J K L

Dip, then curve upward slightly before curving downward on B, D, P, and R.

M M N N O

Keep basic curve subtle.

AVOID:

P Q R S T U

SPEND TIME TRACING THESE LETTERS WITH A LARGE PEN, THEN WRITE YOUR OWN.

V W X Y Z

MODIFIED LOWER-CASE ITALIC
These lower-case letters have the same non-rigid rhythmic line as the free caps. Use them with free caps.

5 mm nib

Hunt's Speedball C-O nib used to write this page.

Use any 5 mm nib.

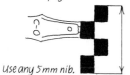

Basic strokes: *4 pen edge widths*

Omit serifs. Down-stroke curves slightly right then left of the basic lower-case letterform.

Maintain 40°-45° pen edge angle.

Ascenders and descenders are approximately 2½ pen edge widths.

Maintain a subtle curve — don't distort!

All letters are one stroke unless otherwise indicated.

Flatten pen for s and stroke 2 of t.

Note:
Serifs are maintained on some letters, such as v, w, x & y.

CURSIVE ITALIC VARIATIONS

Alternative ways of joining into and out of x from the base line.   JOIN 1

ax ix ux · Max Maxine or *Maxine*
add e 2nd stroke of x last

ax

If a 1-stroke e is preferred, lift before e. (avoid e or e or e)   JOIN 3,4

ae ee ie oe ue · Gene Jeannie Reba

a

A 1-stroke e may be alternated with a 2-stroke e.
It is handy to join into the top of e out of o, t, f, v, w & z (Join 5) and out of r (Join 6).

Dexter Gere Irene Joelle Vicente

e

If you prefer to leave top on s when joining from the base line,
then add this letter to Join 8.   *Diagonal to horizontal*

as is us ss · Cassie Gus Luis Susanne

as

You may prefer to lift after o, v, w & x before ascenders.   JOIN 5

ol oh ob ok vl wl wh xl · Harold Tobias

o

You may prefer not to join out of r. If you lift, watch spacing.   JOIN 6

ra re ri ro ru rl rh rb rk rt · Art Earl Eric

r

You may prefer to lift after b & p. Keep spacing even; avoid gaps.   JOIN 7

ba be bi bo bu bb pa pe pi po pu pp · Aphra

b

Debbie Josepha Libby Reuben Sophia

b

You may prefer to lift before a, c, d, g & q from the base line.   JOIN 8

aa ac ad ag aq · Deda Katrina Miguel

a

You may extend serif from base line, then lift. The two letters will appear connected.

Shalonda William S

NO JOIN *Some variations in the no join suggestions may be preferred.*

We read letters by recognizing the shape of the top of each letter (waistline area).

A quick brown fox jumps over the lazy dog

For the sake of legibility, the ascenders must be clear and free of loops. (Loops are not parts of the letters.) Because of this a lift before f is recommended.

Loops on the descenders g, j, q & y sometimes occur when written quickly. These loops below the base line are not as detrimental to legibility as loops above the waist line. You may prefer to join out of g, j, q & y on occasion.

gn ju qu yn · Byron Enrique George Jojo

gn

Use variations of shape, slope, size, and joins to create your own unique handwriting.

SHAPE

o Italic is based on an elliptical shape.

o An expanded elliptical shape or a

o compressed elliptical shape are two variations.

SLOPE

Writing slope may vary from 0° to 15°. Whichever slope you choose be **consistent**.

0° A quick brown fox jumps over the lazy dog.

5° A quick brown fox jumps over the lazy dog.

The writing in this book is at a 5° slope.

10° A quick brown fox jumps over the lazy dog.

15° A quick brown fox jumps over the lazy dog.

SIZE

Cursive italic in this book has a 4mm body height.

Everyone has a writing size which is comfortable.

| 4mm body height | 3mm body height | 2½mm body height |

ITALIC LETTERS: Calligraphy and Handwriting

For everyday writing use notebook paper: wide-ruled or college-ruled. Choose the one that most closely matches your writing size.

9mm *wide-ruled* imaginary waistline at center

notebook paper
4½ mm body height

7½mm *college-ruled* imaginary waistline at center

notebook paper
3¾ mm body height

These timed writings will help improve your writing speed.

The more you write cursive italic, the greater will be your speed. To encourage faster writing follow this procedure.

Write "A quick brown fox jumps over the lazy dog."

WARM-UP

This is a warm-up. Feel comfortable with the words you are writing. (Choose another pangram or sentence if you prefer.)

1. Write pangram at a comfortable rate.

1ST MINUTE

If you finish before a minute is up, start sentence over.
When a minute is up, count the number of words written.

2. Write pangram a litte faster, trying to add 2-3 more words.

2ND MINUTE

When a minute is up, count the number of words written.

3. Write pangram as fast as you can without losing legibility.

3RD MINUTE

When a minute is up, count the number of words written.

4. Write pangram at a comfortable rate.

4TH MINUTE

When a minute is up, count the number of words written & compare with #1.
Chances are your speed of writing increased!

Also try writing with your eyes closed. (Not timed, of course.) You'll be amazed how well you can do.

Fine nib 4mm · Fine nib 3½mm · Fine nib 3mm

5 pen edge widths   4½ pen edge widths   4 pen edge widths

You may prefer to write cursive italic

with chancery italic flourishes on occasion.

The ascenders and descenders are longer

and require lifts before b,f,h,k & l.

A quick brown fox jumps over the lazy dog.

CHAPTER X

&

Z

Design

Design

how to put your calligraphy to work

This chapter presents information on several subjects that will help you use the letterforms that have been introduced throughout this book.

General layout techniques include: three basic page formats, ways to establish formats, line orientation, poster layout ideas, line spacing, and six ways to contrast letters and words with each other (pp. 111-115).

Use italic calligraphy and handwriting for your personal correspondence. Some ideas for letter writing are illustrated on pp. 116 and 117. (If you don't write many letters, now is a good time to begin!)

A handmade book incorporating your calligraphy and handwriting may be designed for personal use or as a special gift. Two designs, the simple handsewn book and the accordion book, are described in this chapter (pp. 118-119).

Improve your skill with the monoline tool & the edged pen by designing your own greeting cards, invitations, certificates, and posters. Gather quotations of others or use your own words — write them out in various ways (pp. 120-121).

Beautiful writing can be a lifelong interest — bring yourself and others pleasure through your newly developed skills.

FORMATS

Three basic choices of format are possible: square, or vertical or horizontal rectangle.

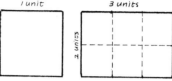

width equals height

SQUARE

height greater than width

VERTICAL RECTANGLE

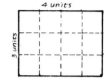

width greater than height

HORIZONTAL RECTANGLE

Some shapes are static (quiet), others are dynamic (active).

STATIC SHAPE: A static shape is formed by repeating identical units. The square is a static shape. Rectangles with ratios of 2:3 and 3:4 are static shapes.

1 unit / 1 unit — **SQUARE**

3 units / 2 units — **2:3 RECTANGLE**

4 units / 3 units — **3:4 RECTANGLE**

DYNAMIC SHAPE: An area of progressively increasing units is referred to as a dynamic shape. The golden rectangle and root rectangles are dynamic shapes.

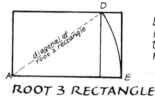

B / diagonal of square / A C — **ROOT 2 RECTANGLE**

Root rectangles begin with a square. The diagonal of the square is equal to the length of a root 2 rectangle.   AB = AC

D / diagonal of root 2 rectangle / A E — **ROOT 3 RECTANGLE**

Diagonal of a root 2 rectangle is equal to the length of a root 3 rectangle.   AD = AE

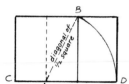

B / diagonal of ½ square / C A D

GOLDEN RECTANGLE
(WHIRLING SQUARE RECTANGLE)

Begin with a square. The diagonal of half of the square plus the length of half the square is equal to the length of a golden rectangle.   AB + AC = CD

Block out the square in a golden rectangle and the remaining area is also a golden rectangle. Add on → a square to form a larger golden rectangle.

An arc described in each square forms a spiral similiar to that of a nautilus shell. (sunflower, pine cone).

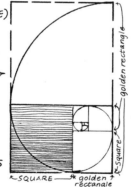

SQUARE / golden rectangle / SQUARE / golden rectangle

NOTE:

To enlarge or reduce a format, use a common diagonal.

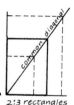

common diagonal

2:3 rectangles

MARGINS

Standard margins are 1 unit at the top, 1½ units at the sides, and 2 units at the bottom. Margins may be arrived at by "eyeballing" (using your inherent sense of balance.)

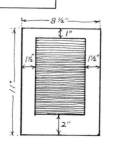

8½" / 1" / 1½" 1½" / 11" / 2"

For example, margins on a 8½" x 11" sheet of paper: 1" at top, 1½ at sides and 2" at bottom.

The text area (shaded area) is approximately 52% of the total area.

LINE ORIENTATION

Lines of writing may be arranged on a page in many ways. Here are some options.

The following layouts are only a beginning – adjust, adapt, experiment.

FLUSH LEFT: All lines begin at left-hand margin. A variation is hanging indentation. *(First line of each paragraph extends left of body of text.)*

flush left

An irregular right margin is usually referred to as "ragged right."

hanging indentation

Paragraph indentation began with the advent of machine-set type. Until then, paragraphs began in the margin or flush left to allow for decorated letters.

FLUSH RIGHT: All lines are flush with right-hand margin.

(The lines of text in most printed books are flush left and flush right.)

flush right

For flush right use technique described for centering, but match last letter of each line with right margin.

CENTERED LINES: The center of each line of writing is placed on the vertical center of the page.

Layout technique: Carefully write out each line of text. Number and cut out each line. Fold and draw line at center. (The center is established by holding up to light and checking that first letter overlaps last letter.) Draw center line on final writing sheet or guide sheet. Use drafting tape to fasten appropriate strip with center line directly above center line of final writing sheet. Then copy below. Repeat process for each line of text. *(This also helps avoid omitting and misspelling words.)*

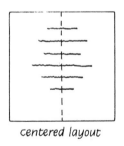

centered layout

CENTERING

rough draft · match center lines

learn to write italic

learn to write italic

final copy

RANDOM CENTERING: Using a vertical line to divide page in half, stagger lines randomly. *(See "Spiders" & "Exciting" layouts on p. 121.)*

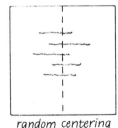

random centering

AVOID:

layouts that pull the reader's eye off the page at a diagonal.

POSTER LAYOUT

The need for a poster arises often, from 1 or 2 words on a line to a complex array of information. If one line is required, center the line on the golden mean (rather than "dead center"). Use cover stock paper or sign board.

Golden Mean

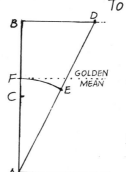

To find golden mean:
1. Establish C halfway on line AB (height of poster).
   AC = CB
2. Measure distance of AC and establish D at top.
   AC = CB = BD
3. Draw diagonal from A to D. Establish E on diagonal using the length of AC.
   AC = CB = BD = DE
4. Measure distance of AE and establish F on line AB (height of poster).
   AE = AF
5. From F draw line parallel to top and bottom.
   Place writing so this golden mean line is at the center of the letters.

---

golden mean

WELCOME

For centering, see line orientation page 112.

When a lot of information is required on a poster use size and form contrasts (see contrasts pages 114-115). The WHAT or WHO should be written with the largest letters (size) and often in capitals (form). Next in importance is usually WHEN, followed closely by WHERE. Lastly, details such as cost may be written with the smallest letters, using lowercase. Allow generous margins.

WHAT or WHO
WHEN
WHERE
Details and other information

A centered format is the most formal. (see line orientation, page 112)

WHEN
MORE WHEN

WHO golden mean

WHERE
MORE WHERE

Details & information

A flush left line orientation is the quickest. (see page 112) For more emphasis on WHO or WHAT center on the golden mean.

LINE SPACING

STANDARD SPACING: Ascenders and descenders barely touch, but do not overlap.

practice your handwriting

BASIC ITALIC
standard spacing

calligraphy is creative

FORMAL ITALIC
standard spacing

OPEN SPACING: Additional space occurs between ascenders and de-cenders. (Because of the flourished serifs, open spacing works well with the chancery hand.)

this is a

sample of

open spacing

CHANCERY ITALIC

TIGHT SPACING: Very little space occurs between the lines of writing. (The words should remain legible.)

this is a sample of tight-ly packed letters — can you read this writing?

BASIC ITALIC

BASIC CONTRASTS

There are many ways in which letters, words, and lines may be contrasted with each other. Basic contrasts include size, weight, form, color, direction, and texture.

SIZE: To achieve a contrast in size, use different pen nib widths. Maintain a standard 5 pen-edge width body height with each nib.

FINE AND BROAD NIBS

Achieve a contrast of size by changing pen nib widths

n n Size of letters changes as size of nibs changes.

BROAD NIB   FINE NIB

Make a strong contrast. For example, use a broad nib (2 mm) with a fine nib (1mm or smaller).

WEIGHT: A lightweight letter is characterized by a narrow line and a large counter; a heavyweight

FINE AND BROAD NIBS

light heavy weight weight

letter is characterized by a wide line and a small counter.

ɔn ɜn *Size of letter does not change, weight of line changes.*

FORM: Shape is a synonym for form. The most elementary contrast in calligraphy is between the letters of the alphabet, since each has a different form or shape. Contrast of form in design is the contrast of different letter shapes or scripts.

(This book is concerned with one script – italic.)

COLOR: Experiment with colored inks & watercolors to enhance your calligraphic layouts. *(Consult Albers, Dair, and Itten in the bibliography.)*

DIRECTION: When dealing with words, we have a left-to-right horizontal orientation. When changing the direction of writing, use a strong letterform for contrast.

(Generally, writing on the left side of the page reads from bottom to top and on the right from top to bottom.)

<u>Do</u> avoid stacking letters ᴸᴵᴷᴱ ᵀᴴᴵˢ

TEXTURE: Texture occurs wherever there are enough letters in a given area to form a pattern. The shape, weight, & spacing of the letters determine the texture and weave of a layout.

layout demonstrating size and weight fine nib at 12 and 3 pen edge widths

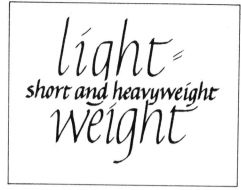

light short and heavyweight weight

plain caps contrasted with formal lower-case

contrasting contrasting contrasting
FORM
contrasting contrasting contrasting contrasting contrasting

contrast of direction

DIRECTION At times it is reasonable to change the direction of your writing. But do use this technique with caution. DIRECTION

monoline tool · caps and lower-case

TEXTURE TEXTURE TEXTURE
texture texture texture texture texture
texture texture texture texture texture
TEXTURE TEXTURE TEXTURE

Read your text — it will help you determine the basic contrasts to use when designing your layout.

PERSONAL CORRESPONDENCE

chancery italic · Gothic flourish on R and B · edged pens

Rich

Just a note to thank you
for sending me the information about
cutting pens from cattail reeds.
I hope to see you soon.

Brenda

18 · XI · 84

One of the anticipations of each week-
day is checking the mail. How grand
it is when we receive a handwritten
message from a friend. You can
bring joy into the lives of others
with a cheery note or letter — and
you can practice your calligraphy
at the same time. Surprise a friend
with your words!

formal italic & italic handwriting · edged pens

Sometimes
messages
can be written
at random.

Not all of your
correspondence
has to be
designed the
same.

Ann

Put
a surprise in the
envelope by designing
your own format.

edged pen quote · monoline message

There's more to it than just wiggling your fingers and out come the letters

Dear Bev,
I under-
stand you're
a beginning
calligrapher.
TERRIFIC!
One of the
best ways to
exercise your
skill is
by writing
notes and
letters to
your friends.
You might
write a short
quote with an
edged pen, then write
the text
with a mono-
line tool, as I
have done here.

HOWARD GLASSER

Love, Barbara
15 · IX · 84

quoted with permission of Howard Glasser

compressed vertical caps for caption · monoline tool for all writing

letters. Write on! • Dear Reader, Not all letters have to be written on

WRITE LETTERS ON LONG STRIPS

sheets of paper. Sometimes print shops will sell or give you endcuts.

Use them for

standard sizes

monoline message in background - vertical caps · edged pen text

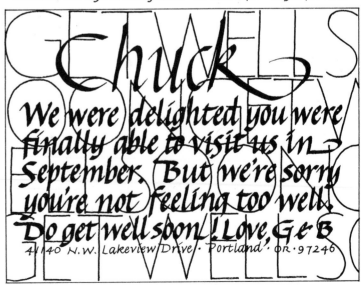

Chuck
We were delighted you were
finally able to visit us in
September. But we're sorry
you're not feeling too well.
Do get well soon!! Love, G & B
41140 N.W. Lakeview Drive · Portland · OR · 97246

SPIRAL WRITING

For an unusual design for a letter try a spiral! Find the center of sheet (a quick way: fold in half and crease lightly) & draw a line horizontally at center. Establish A at center of line. One half inch to the right of A, establish B. Place point of compass at A & the lead of compass an inch or so from the left edge of paper and draw a semicircle on top half of sheet. Next, move point of compass to B & line up lead of compass with line just drawn (tighten compass slightly to adjust). Each semicircle on the top has A as its center, & each semicircle on the bottom has B as its center. Continue spiral to center.

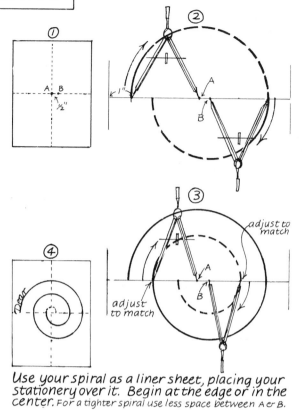

Use your spiral as a liner sheet, placing your stationery over it. Begin at the edge or in the center. For a tighter spiral use less space between A & B.

ENVELOPE DESIGNS

Design your own envelope by using a commercial envelope for a pattern. Cut your envelopes from plain paper, gift wrap paper, or large magazine covers. For the last two papers, use a self-sticking label for the address & attach the stamp with glue.

Mike
4602 S.W. Lakeview Drive · Portland · OR · 97206
Hilton

Margaret
420 JFK BLVD
PHILADELPHIA
PA · 17614

HAPPY BIRTHDAY HAPPY BIRTHDAY
Arlene Robs
723 S. Elm
Boise, ID 11136
BIRTHDAY

Darla Jean Cramer
48321 Lee Avenue
Bloomsburg · PA · 17121

Gilham
7061 West Alpine
Peoria, IL 43072

Note:
The state and zip code should be written on the same line.

2763 N. Beach Drive
ROGER BAIN
Catalina · CA · 98761

MARTIN · MAR *Beverly* TIN · MARTIN · MARTIN
572 POLK AVENUE
MIAMI · FL · 12345

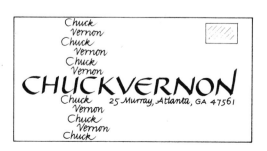
Chuck Vernon Chuck Vernon Chuck Vernon
CHUCKVERNON
Chuck 25 Murray, Atlanta, GA 47561
Vernon Chuck Vernon Chuck

SIMPLE HANDSEWN BOOK
The simple handsewn book can be a useful place to keep notes, write a journal, or keep other handwritten information. It can be used as a gift with quotations, stories, or poems written out on its pages.

Begin with 8 sheets of 8½" x 11" bond paper. (8 sheets will make a 32-page book.) Fold each sheet in half and place one inside the other. This group of sheets is called a signature. Choose a heavier weight paper (cover stock) for the cover - 8½" x 11¼". Fold and place outside signature. Secure group of sheets with paper clips or clothespins. Poke 5 holes at the

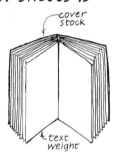

cover stock

text weight

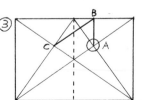

spine

spine with an awl or darning needle, first one in the center, then two other holes evenly spaced on either side. Sew as shown with thread & darning needle.

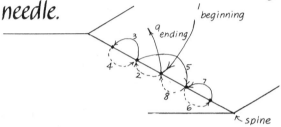

beginning

ending

spine

Be sure thread is pulled taut and that beginning & ending thread are on either side of center thread (5). Then make square knot. Trim ends of thread to an inch or so.

THE CANON · DESIGN FOR 2-PAGE SPREAD · TEXT AREA & MARGINS

①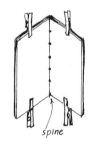

Draw diagonals of unit of 2 pages.

② Draw diagonals to top center.

③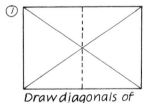

From intersection of 2 diagonals on right (A) draw perpendicular line from A to B, then connect to intersection of diagonals on left at C.

④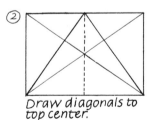

Point at which B C line intersects diagonal of right side establishes top, side and bottom margins.

This page design for books was used throughout the late Middle Ages and early Renaissance.

It was rediscovered by Jan Tschichold, a Swiss designer. It can be worked on any vertical format.

gutter margin

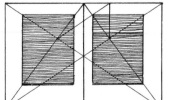

Note gutter margin (center) is the same width as the side margins and the bottom margin is twice the height of the top margin.

Text area of 2-page spread (shaded area)

THE ACCORDION BOOK

The accordion book design originated in the Orient and is composed of a continuous folded sheet of paper enclosed between 2 covers. It may be constructed in any size – from very small to very large – and is a handsome design for a booklet or a special greeting card.

SUPPLIES

- cover board (cardboard, poster board, illustration board)
- cloth or paper for cover
- adding machine tape or pieces of paper joined to make a long strip
- ribbon or cord for ties
- library paste, gluestick, Sobo, or white water-soluble glue (diluted)

(Avoid rubber cement as it comes through the paper after several months.)

PROCEDURE

- Determine spacing of message on rough draft to determine length of strip.
- Fold strip in equal sections – use any EVEN number of rectangles or squares.
- Write final copy.

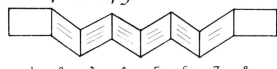

- Cut 2 covers ⅛" to ¼" larger on all sides than folded strip.

(When working with children, use ¼" to ½" larger covers on all sides for ease in handling.)

- Cut 2 pieces of cloth or paper for cover ½" to ⅝" larger on all sides than the cover board.
- Apply glue to cover board & attach cloth or paper to each board.
- Miter corners, then glue & overlap edges – steps 1, 2, and 3ᵃ or 3ᵇ.

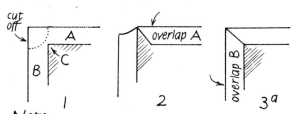

Note:
Curve corner when cutting, but do <u>not</u> cut to corner (C), or a cloth corner <u>will</u> fray.

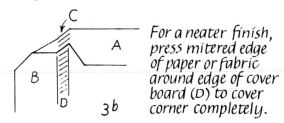

For a neater finish, press mitered edge of paper or fabric around edge of cover board (D) to cover corner completely.

- Glue ribbon across horizontal center of inside of back cover.
- Glue last rectangle of accordion pages to the inside of back cover <u>over the ribbon</u> – leave an equal cover margin on all 4 sides.
- Glue front cover to first rectangle, carefully squaring it with back cover. (If cover design has directional pattern, match before gluing.)

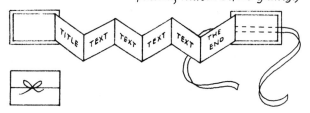

CARDS · CERTIFICATES · INVITATIONS

GREETING CARD: To make a greeting card for a business size envelope, 4⅛" x 8½" (10.5 cm x 24 cm), you will need: scissors · 24" (61 cm) thread or yarn · needle · ruler · paperclips · 1 sheet of lightweight paper cut to 7½" x 8¾" (19 cm x 22 cm) for inside card · 1 sheet of mediumweight colored paper cut to 8" x 9" (20 cm x 23 cm) for cover of card.

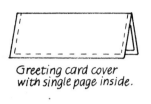

Greeting card cover with single page inside.

Stitch as shown.

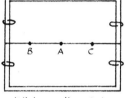

With needle, establish holes at ABC.

flush left layout · free caps · handwriting

· SUPER NEIGHBOR AWARD ·
is hereby bestowed upon

FRAN BYERS

for her neighborly efforts
beyond the call of duty

WITH THANKS FROM ALL OF US

Dated at Denver · Colorado · USA
this 15th day of October · 1984

Gertrude E. Schnackschneider
CHAIRPERSON

hanging indentation · free caps · modified italic

EMPLOYEE
Publications Department · Glenn Manufacturing Company, Inc.
OF THE MONTH

for making a unique contribution to our organization

TODD ANDREWS

has been selected by his peers
as the employee of the month
for March, 1984.

SELECTION COMMITTEE   _____   _____
_____   _____
_____   _____

centered layout · chancery italic

You are invited to a reception for
Louis and Annette Kaufman

6:00 to 7:45 P.M., November 10

Community Music Center

3350 S.E. Francis, Portland

centered layout · free caps · modified italic lower-case

Ann Linzy and Bill Kemnitzer
would like their families and friends to gather
for a wedding reception celebrating love and happiness
on Saturday, the twentieth of November
nineteen hundred eighty-two
from four to seven in the evening
Quinn's Inn
4210 Southwest Macadam
Rochester, Michigan

GENERAL LAYOUTS

centered horizontal format · chancery italic and free caps · contrast of size & form

For all that has been
THANKS
for all that will be
YES

DAG HAMMARSKJØLD

centered horizontal format · chancery italic

It's got to be the going, not the getting there, that's good.

Here are layouts demonstrating some of the letter-forms and design techniques presented in this book. Collect quotations that mean something to you, then write them for yourself and for your friends. Design a simple poster for an event — a meeting, a concert, a sale. The fun begins when you put your calligraphy to work!

vertical format · tight spacing random centering · formal italic

don't worry spiders, I keep house casually

vertical format · hanging indentation · contrast of 4 sizes · formal italic with basic capitals

Senior Cello Recital
an afternoon program of
BACH · BEETHOVEN · SAINT-SAËNS
Gregory
Dubay

Student of Naomi Blumberg

Margaret Moore, piano

Community Music Center
3350 S.E. Francis Street · Portland

Saturday · May 23 · 2 P.M.

horizontal format · random centering · contrast of size and form · free caps and modified lower-case

One of the advantages
of being disorderly
is that one is constantly making
EXCITING
discoveries

Note:
This book was entirely handwritten actual size
except for reductions on pp. 2, 6, 117, 120 & 121.

GLOSSARY

ASCENDER · The part of a letter that extends above the body height.

BASE LINE · The line on which letters "sit"; bottom line of body height. (Sometimes called writing line.)

BASIC ITALIC · A form of unjoined writing using italic letters without entrance or exit serifs.

BODY HEIGHT · The distance between base line & waist line. (Sometimes called "x height".)

BRANCHING LINE · An imaginary line in the center of the body height.

CALLIGRAPHY · Beautiful or elegant writing; also the art of producing such writing. The letters are generally unjoined and often written with the edged tool. Italic calligraphy is one type of formal hand lettering or writing.

CAPITAL LETTER · A letter in the series A, B, C, rather than a, b, c. (Sometimes called upper case, large letters, or caps.) Synonym: majuscule.

CHANCERY ITALIC · During the 15th and 16th centuries, the official handwriting of the chancery, the office where papal documents were kept.

COUNTER · The open area within a letter.

CROSSBAR · A horizontal line, second stroke of f and t.

CURSIVE ITALIC · A form of joined writing using italic letters with entrance and exit serifs. [Medieval Latin SCRIPTA CURSIVA–"flowing script"–from Latin CURSUS, past participle of CURRERE–"to run."] Four characteristics of a cursive hand are compressed (elliptical) forms, slight slope, fluent (branching for one-stroke letters) and joined letters.

DESCENDER · The part of a letter that extends below the base line and the body height.

DIAGONAL · A line from lower left to upper right (as used in joins & letter shapes) or a line from upper left to lower right (as used in letter shapes).

DOWNSTROKE · A line from top to bottom following letter slope angle.

ELLIPTICAL SHAPE · A line following a compressed circular shape or elongated circle (as in o).

HORIZONTAL · A line extending from left to right parallel to base line & waist line.

INTERSPACE · An area between letters within words.

ITALIC · A script originating in Italy in the late 15th and early 16th centuries. It is a slightly sloped, compressed, and fluent version of the 15th century humanist script. Italic was first called humanist cursive.

ITALIC HANDWRITING · A system of writing for everyday use incorporating both an unjoined form of writing (basic italic) and a cursive form of writing (cursive italic).

LETTER · **SHAPE** · The correct form of a capital or lower-case letter.
   SIZE · The height or length of a letter.
   SLOPE · The slant of a letter.
   SPACING · The distance between letters in words.
   SPEED · The rate of writing.
   STROKES · The lines without lifts used to write a letter.

LOWER-CASE LETTER · A letter in the series a, b, c, rather than A, B, C. (Sometimes called small letters.) [From the printer's practice of keeping the small letters in the lower of a pair of type cases or drawers.] Synonym: minuscule.

PEN EDGE ANGLE · The angle of the edge of the pen nib in relation to the base line.

SERIF · An entrance or exit stroke of a letter.

UPPER CASE · See CAPITAL LETTER. [From the printer's practice of keeping the large letters in the upper of a pair of type cases or drawers.]

VERTICAL · A line from top to bottom following the slope line.

WAIST LINE · The top line of the body height.

BIBLIOGRAPHY

Albers, Josef. INTERACTION OF COLOR. New Haven: Yale University Press, 1963.

Anderson, Charles. LETTERING, expanded ed. New York: Van Nostrand Reinhold, 1982.

Anderson, Donald M. THE ART OF WRITTEN FORMS. New York: Holt, Rinehart and Winston, 1969.

Benson, John Howard. THE FIRST WRITING BOOK: AN ENGLISH TRANSLATION & FACSIMILE TEXT OF ARRIGHI'S Operina, THE FIRST MANUAL OF THE CHANCERY HAND. New Haven: Yale University Press, 1955.

CALLIGRAPHY — THE GOLDEN AGE AND ITS MODERN REVIVAL. Portland, OR: Portland Art Association, 1958.

Catich, Edward M. THE ORIGIN OF THE SERIF. Davenport, IA: Catfish Press, 1968.

Dair, Carl. DESIGN WITH TYPE. Toronto: University of Toronto Press, 1967.

Degering, Hermann. LETTERING: MODES OF WRITING IN WESTERN EUROPE FROM ANTIQUITY TO THE END OF THE EIGHTEENTH CENTURY. New York: Taplinger/Pentalic, 1978.

Dubay, Inga, and Barbara Getty. ITALIC HANDWRITING SERIES, BOOKS D, E, F, G, and INSTRUCTIONAL MANUAL. Portland, OR: Portland State University, Division of Continuing Education, 1980.

Fairbank, Alfred. THE STORY OF HANDWRITING. London: Faber & Faber, 1970.

Fairbank, Alfred, and R. W. Hunt. HUMANISTIC SCRIPT OF THE FIFTEENTH AND SIXTEENTH CENTURIES. Oxford: Oxford University Press, 1960.

Gelb, I. J., A STUDY OF WRITING. Chicago: University of Chicago Press, 1963.

Getty, Barbara, and Inga Dubay. ITALIC HANDWRITING SERIES, BOOKS A, B, C, G & IM. Portland, OR: Portland State University, Division of Continuing Education, 1980.

Gourdie, Tom. ITALIC HANDWRITING. New York: Taplinger, 1976.

Gray, Bill. LETTERING TIPS FOR ARTISTS, GRAPHIC DESIGNERS, AND CALLIGRAPHERS. Van Nostrand Reinhold, 1980.

Gürtler, Andre. THE DEVELOPMENT OF THE ROMAN ALPHABET. Basle: Bildungsverband Schweizerischer Buchdrucker.

Hambidge, Jay. THE ELEMENTS OF DYNAMIC SYMMETRY. New York: Dover Publications. 1967.

Harvard, Stephen. AN ITALIC COPYBOOK; THE CATANEO MANUSCRIPT. New York: Pentalic, 1981.

Hayes, James. THE ROMAN LETTER. Chicago: Lakeside Press.

Itten, Johannes. THE ELEMENTS OF COLOR. New York: Van Nostrand Reinhold, 1970.

Jackson, Donald. THE STORY OF WRITING. New York: Taplinger, 1981.

Jarman, Christopher J. THE DEVELOPMENT OF HANDWRITING SKILLS. London: Basil Blackwell, 1979.

Johnson, Pauline. CREATIVE BOOKBINDING. Seattle: University of Washington Press, 1963.

Johnston, Edward. WRITING AND ILLUMINATING AND LETTERING. New York: Taplinger/Pentalic, 1975.

Lehman, Charles L. HANDWRITING MODELS FOR SCHOOLS. Portland, OR: Alcuin Press, 1976.

Lindegren, Erik. ABC OF LETTERING AND PRINTING TYPES. New York: Pentalic, 1976.

Mann, William. LETTERING AND LETTERING DISPLAY. New York: Van Nostrand Reinhold, 1974.

Moorehouse, A.C. THE TRIUMPH OF THE ALPHABET: A HISTORY OF WRITING. New York: Henry Schuman, 1953.

Petersen, Karen, and J.J. Wilson. WOMEN ARTISTS: RECOGNITION & REAPPRAISAL FROM THE EARLY MIDDLE AGES TO THE TWENTIETH CENTURY. New York: New York University Press, 1976.

Reynolds, Lloyd J. ITALIC CALLIGRAPHY AND HANDWRITING. New York: Pentalic, 1969.

Roland, Benjamin. CAVE TO RENAISSANCE. Boston: Little, Brown, 1965.

Studley, Vance. LEFT-HANDED CALLIGRAPHY. New York: Van Nostrand Reinhold, 1979.

Svaren, Jacqueline. WRITTEN LETTERS, expanded and revised ed. New York: Taplinger/Pentalic, 1982.

Thompson, Edward Maunde, A HANDBOOK OF GREEK & LATIN PALAEOGRAPHY. Chicago: Ares, 1980.

Tschichold, Jan. "Non-Arbitrary Proportions of Page and Type Area." In CALLIGRAPHY AND PALAEOGRAPHY, edited by A.S. Osley, 179–92. London: Faber and Faber, 1965.

TWO THOUSAND YEARS OF CALLIGRAPHY. Totowa, NJ: Rowman and Littlefield, 1965.

Ullman, B.L. ANCIENT WRITING AND ITS INFLUENCE. New York: Cooper Square Publishers, 1963.

Von Eckardt, Wolf. "The All But Lost Art of Handwriting." HORIZON. September, 1959, pp. 124–128.

Wallbank, T. Walter, and Alastair M. Taylor. CIVILIZATION, PAST AND PRESENT. Chicago: Scott Foresman, 1949.

INDEX

Sample Ruled Page · 4mm